NEW AGE MENACE

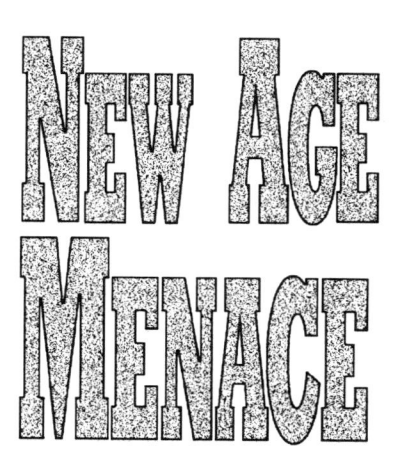

NEW AGE MENACE

THE SECRET WAR AGAINST THE FOLLOWERS OF CHRIST

DAVID N. BALMFORTH

Copyright © 1996 By
HORIZON PUBLISHERS & DISTRIBUTORS, INC.

All rights reserved.
Reproduction in whole or any parts thereof in any form
or by any media without written permission is prohibited.

Second Printing: March, 1998

International Standard Book Number:
0-88290-535-X

Horizon Publishers' Catalog and Order Number:
1067

Printed and distributed
in the United States of America by

Horizon Publishers
& Distributors, Incorporated

Mailing Address:
P.O. Box 490
Bountiful, Utah 84011-0490

Street Address:
50 South 500 West
Bountiful, Utah 84010

Local Phone: (801) 295-9451
WATS (toll free): 1 (800) 453-0812
FAX: (801) 295-0196
Internet: www.horizonpublishers.com

DEDICATION

To the dedicated lovers of liberty who have come forth in these latter-days who were held in reserve to come forth in this chosen period to preserve and maintain the heritage and birthright of freedom set forth by the Lord.

TABLE OF CONTENTS

FOREWORD 9
Chapter 1
THE NATURE OF THE BATTLE 11
 A World Ripe in Wickedness 11
 The Wicked Days of Noah Revisited 13
 Likening the Scriptures to Ourselves 14
 What Can You Do? 15
 Prophecies About This Day 16
 Apathy is the Enemy 17

Chapter 2
WHAT IS THE NEW AGE MOVEMENT? 23
 The "Plan" to Overthrow Christianity 24
 New Age/Occult Practices 25
 Satanic Spirits Inspire New-Age Thought 26
 The "Aquarian Conspiracy" 27
 Rejection of Jesus Christ Is a New Age Doctrine 29
 New Age Symbols Engulf the World 36
 Loosely Structured Or Very Organized 36
 Latter-day Saints Need To Become Informed 44

Chapter 3
"THE PLAN"—THE NEW WORLD RELIGION 47
 Some Christians View LDS with Hostility 51

Chapter 4
THE EXISTENCE OF SATAN AND HIS SPIRIT FOLLOWERS 55
 A Conversation with Lucifer 56

Chapter 5
WITCHCRAFT, A NEW AGE RELIGION 61
 Witchcraft and Illuminati Ties to the
  New Age Movement 63
 The Organization and Religion of the Illuminati 64
 The American Illuminati 66

A Managed Crisis: Strikes, Riots,
   Revolution and U.S. Takeover Planned 67
Are Christians Such a Threat to the New Age? 72

Chapter 6

SATAN'S SYMBOLS AND MUSIC 83
   The Pentagram and Hexagram 84
   The Goat Head Pentagram 84
   The Ankh 87
   The Yin/Yang 87
   The "Peace" Symbol 87
   The Unicorn's Horn 88
   Satanic Forms of Music 88
   Music Affects Behavior 89
   Rock Music 94
   Rock Lyrics 95
   New Age Music 97

Chapter 7

A NEW BIBLE PLANNED FOR MANKIND 103
   New Age Holistic Health 108
   Hidden New Age Seminars .109
   Spiritualism, Witchcraft and Astrology 111
   Astrology and Spiritualism 112

Chapter 8

WHO IS LORD MAITREYA? 117
   The Year 2000 and the Age of Aquarius 124

Chapter 9

WHAT IS THE RESPONSIBILITY OF THE SAINTS? 127
   What Can the Saints Do to Prepare? 133
   What Can Be Done? 136
END NOTES 139
BIBLIOGRAPHY 149
INDEX 157
ABOUT THE AUTHOR 171

FOREWORD

This book came about as a result of the author's research and study into various writings and publications of New Age thought. The growing influence of the "New Age Movement" across virtually all aspects of our lives has become a real concern. Its power, dominion and control is spreading all across the world at an alarming speed.

I have found that very few Saints are aware of the New Age Movement and the immediate dangers it poses in its push for an oppressive world religion and government hostile to religious values and true liberties. Many of the Christian ideals that this nation was founded upon are already being rapidly undermined and discarded. Few Saints realize that this is part of a concerted, organized effort by organizations bound together by common philosophies, the whole of which is called the New Age Movement. Likewise, many Saints do not see how this movement is poised to fulfill numerous prophecies as a great arm of Satan's "great and abominable church."

The oppressive New Age agenda is not "out there" in some obscured think tank, but is likely part of your community's affairs, public education programs, and popular entertainment. You have the ability to fight Satan's oppressive agenda—this book will help you recognize his programs and tactics in several crucial areas.

Taking very seriously the admonition by the Lord in D & C 88:81, "... *it becometh every man who hath been warned to warn his neighbor*," I have tried to make known some of the dangers that are quietly spreading throughout this nation and the world. It is my wish that this book will bring a knowledge and understanding of some of the New Age movement's very real dangers and ultimately prove a blessing to you, your family, your posterity and our country.

David N. Balmforth

Chapter One

THE NATURE OF THE BATTLE

A powerful spiritual and social revolution in traditional morals, religion and belief in the existence of God is sweeping across America and the rest of the world. There is talk of a new world religion based on mysticism and the occult that will eventually encompass all others. This may have come about in part because of widespread disillusionment with orthodox Christianity and religion in general. The scriptures speak of the days before the second coming of the Savior as being filled with rebellion against God and of a great apostasy or "falling away" from his revealed word. Are these powerful forces of change we are experiencing destined to bring about the prophesied scriptural tribulations set forth in the Bible and Book of Mormon that are to happen in "the Latter-days?"

This book will examine these powerful forces, their objectives and how we may be affected by their emergence on the world scene.

A World Ripe in Wickedness

In 2 Timothy, Paul warns that the last days will be filled with apostasy and perilous times:

> For men shall be lovers of their own selves, covetous, boasters, proud, blasphemers, disobedient to parents, unthankful, unholy,

> Without natural affection, trucebreakers, false accusers, incontinent, fierce, despisers of those that are good,
>
> Traitors, heady, highminded, lovers of pleasures more than lovers of God;
>
> . . . Evil men and seducers shall wax worse and worse, deceiving, and being deceived.
>
> . . . For the time will come when they will not endure sound doctrine; but after their own lusts shall they . . . turn away their ears from the truth, and shall be turned unto fables (2 Timothy 3:2-4, 13; 4:3-4).

The Lord warned that during the days preceding his second coming, or "in the last days, . . . upon all the lands of the earth, behold, they will be drunken with iniquity and all manner of abominations—" (2 Nephi 27:1). He has said that "the whole earth shall be in commotion" (D & C 45:26). There will be new diseases and plagues, formerly unheard of, that will assail mankind, and "a desolating sickness shall cover the land" (D & C 45:31). It will be a time of "false Christs, and false prophets," deceptions, and great "signs and wonders; insomuch that, if it were possible, they shall deceive the very elect" (Matthew 24:24).

In 3 Nephi the Lord provides this vivid description of the spiritual state of many in the latter days:

> . . . the Gentiles shall sin against my gospel, and shall reject the fullness of my gospel, and shall be lifted up in the pride of their hearts above all nations, and above all the people of the whole earth, and shall be filled with all manner of lyings, and of deceits, and of mischiefs, and all manner of hypocrisy, and murders, and priestcrafts, and whoredoms, and of secret abominations; . . . (3 Nephi 16:10).

A prophet of God declared that these are the prophesied days of wickedness. At baccalaureate services in the Ricks College field house on May 7, 1971, President Joseph Fielding Smith declared:

> There is more sin and evil in the world now than there has been at any time since the day of Noah, when the Lord felt dis-

posed to destroy the world by a flood so that He could send His spirit children to earth in a better and more righteous environment. This is the day which Christ said that 'iniquity shall abound.'[1]

Earlier that same year, then-Apostle Spencer W. Kimball declared:

> Our world is now much the same as it was in the days of the Nephite prophet who said: '. . . if it were not for the prayers of the righteous . . . ye would even now be visited with utter destruction' (Alma 10:22). Of course, there are many upright and faithful who live all the commandments and whose lives and prayers keep the world from utter destruction.[2]

To many, the steady degeneration of our world's moral climate since these declarations is obvious; these declarations should be much more ominous now.

The Wicked Days of Noah Revisited

The unequaled wickedness in the days of Noah enjoys a close, albeit twisted, parallel in New Age dogma. They reverently speak of a highly-evolved civilization called Atlantis that was utterly destroyed in our earth's prehistory. Believers say that its lost knowledge and mysteries are now being rediscovered and they are reintroducing them into our society.

These "discoveries" are not welcomed by followers of Jesus Christ. Biblical researcher Dwight L. Kinman states:

> Occult tradition reveals that the world, prior to the flood, had a unified global government of ten regions called Atlantis. Atlantis is the New Age secret code word for the advanced civilization before the flood. In the day of Noah it was a demonized society that God had to destroy.[3]

How interesting it is that in this age, where wickedness exceeds that of Noah's age, occult "secrets" from the pre-flood era are making their way back into modern society. Just as the Nephites and Lamanites sought out the ancient secret oaths whenever wickedness increased, today's growing love affair with New Age organizations is a revival of ancient satanic secrets which flourish among the wicked and the gullible.

The scriptures state that Satan is the mastermind of these problems, for he has "sought the misery of all mankind." It is Satan, "the father of all lies" (2 Nephi 2:18), who desires "to deceive and blind men, and to lead them captive," (Moses 4:4, JST Genesis 3:5) and "who hath caused man to commit murder from the beginning" (Ether 8:25).

God sent the flood because society had reached the point in its depravity, ungodliness and mocking that there was no hope of redemption for those the flood engulfed (See Genesis 6:12-13, 2 Peter 2:5). All moral restraints had been removed. In these last days, much of the world has become as wicked as these people were!

Paul instructed the early Church about the days preceding the Second Coming, giving counsel pertinent to the Saints of today:

> . . . be not soon shaken in mind, or be troubled by letter, except ye receive it from us; neither by spirit, nor by word, as that the day of Christ is at hand. . . .
>
> Yea, the Lord, even Jesus, whose coming is not until after there cometh a falling away, by the working of Satan with all power, and signs and lying wonders, . . .
>
> Therefore, brethren, stand fast, and hold the traditions which ye have been taught, whether by word, or our epistle (2 Thessalonians 2:2, 3, 9, 13 ,15; Joseph Smith Translation).

Likening the Scriptures to Ourselves

Church leaders continually remind the Saints that the Book of Mormon was prepared for this day and that they should faithfully study it throughout their lives. One reason for this is that the Book of Mormon gives insight into the workings of both God and

Satan among entire civilizations. Mormon declared that the gold plates could not contain "the hundredth" of the doings of the people (Words of Mormon 1:5). He therefore had to be selective, providing only what would be the most needed:

> Behold, I speak unto you as if ye were present, and yet ye are not. But behold, Jesus Christ hath shown you unto me, and I know your doing.
>
> Behold, I speak unto you as though I spake from the dead, for I know that ye shall have my words (Mormon 8:35, 9:30).

Having seen this day, Mormon included accounts to help today's Saints with modern problems. The Book of Mormon contains numerous accounts of secret combinations, wars, persecutions of the faithful, and of churches built up to get gain. The prominence of these accounts indicates that one should expect to find the same things in this day.

If the scriptures are to be likened unto ourselves, then it is necessary to look around and see what in this world parallels Nephite history. Organizations under the massive umbrella of the New Age movement combine the craftiness of Amalikiah (Alma 47), the persuasiveness of Nehor (Alma 1) and Korihor (Alma 30), with the murderous self-righteousness of the Ammonihahites (Alma 14). Its followers occupy high levels of government (Helaman 14) and will eventually invite all to either join them or be conquered (3 Nephi 3:7-8, Revelation 13:15). The New Age movement is a result of wicked people who have resurrected the ancient "covenants, agreements . . . and secret combinations" (Alma 37:27) whose author is Satan.

What Can You Do?

Many of Satan's evils are so well-disguised that they are best discerned spiritually. Because the Lord requires us to ponder things in our minds (D & C 9:8-9), this book will hopefully provide food for thought. The author encourages the reader to think about whether the evils described in this book exist within his own community or family. Perhaps the reader has even unwittingly accepted some New Age philosophy or practice himself.

In any case, please ask the Lord what to do about these dangers. The New Age movement is not something that can only be fought by politicians and people in high places of power. It is something that affects individuals—family, friends, members of one's ward and stake. As widespread as the New Age movement is, most can hope to fight its influence only in their corner of the world. Please ponder these words, as well as the words of the prophets, and ask the Lord what to do.

Prophecies About This Day

If there be any doubt regarding the urgency of these problems, one need only read the prophecies regarding this day. They teach that Satan will be more powerful and organized, more effective in his approach and better disguised than at any point in the history of the world.

Ancient prophets, including Paul, John, Nephi and Mormon repeatedly warn of the need to be vigilant in protecting one's freedoms and religious heritage. Nephi and John warn of a gigantic satanic organization that will completely cover the earth and have dominion among all nations, kindreds, tongues and people. This organization will count among its membership the entire human race, except those few who remain true to "the Church of the Lamb of God" (1 Nephi 14:10). This great conspiratorial organization desires to overthrow the freedom of all lands, nations, and countries (Ether 8:25) and will make war against the Saints and slay them (1 Nephi 13:5, Revelation 17:6). It will pursue its satanic course until it obtains power over all nations (Revelation 13:7).

Should an evil organization of this magnitude deserve the Saints' attention? Can this immense entity, which desires to take away the freedoms and religion of the Saints, be dismissed as of no concern? Shouldn't the Saints be committed to gaining the necessary knowledge so that they can recognize it and understand how to fight it?

Apathy is the Enemy

While ancient and modern prophets have continually admonished the Saints to be aware of the workings of Satan, a portion of the Church has always been more comfortable pretending that there is no enemy at the doorstep. The Lord is displeased with those who refuse to acknowledge Satan's work, allowing it to go unchecked:

> *Therefore, wo be unto him that is at ease in Zion!*
> *Wo be unto him that crieth: All is well!*
> (2 Nephi 28:22, 24-25).

The author would hope that the dangers outlined in this book do not fall on deaf ears. It is hoped that the reader will recognize various evil influences of the New Age so that he or she may counteract them in his or her community, family, and personal life. New Age leaders desire to create one religion and one government, converting or destroying all who stand in the way.

Elder Henry D. Moyle declared that any person or organization that would inhibit freedom deserves attention:

> All we have to do is just to examine any movement that may be brought into our midst whether it be social or political or what not, and if it has the earmarks of an attempt to deprive us in the slightest respect of our free agency, we should avoid it as we would avoid immorality or anything else that is vicious. I am sure that free agency is as necessary for our eternal salvation as is our virtue. And just as we guard our virtue with our lives, so should we guard our free agency.[4]

The Lord commanded the Saints to "contend against no church, save it be the church of the devil" (D & C 18:20). This emphasizes the importance the Lord puts on recognizing, fighting, and slowing the works of the devil and his organization. But fighting Satan can be difficult, for he lays many traps. Satan is careful to not wake the Saints as he plunders their freedoms little by little. Some of the Saints show so little caution that they unwittingly support destructive practices. Elder Marion G. Romney gave this warning to the Priesthood:

> There was no guarantee that the devil will not deceive a lot of men who hold the Priesthood. . . .
>
> Free agency is the principle against which Satan waged his war in heaven. It is still the front on which he makes his most furious, devious, and persistent attacks . . .
>
> You see, at the time he was cast out of heaven, his objective was (and still is) "to deceive and to blind men, and to lead them captive at his will." This he effectively does to as many as will not hearken unto the voice of God. *His main attack is still on free agency.* When he can get men to yield their agency, he has them well on the way to captivity.
>
> We who hold the Priesthood must beware concerning ourselves, that we do not fall into the traps he lays to rob us of our freedom. We must be careful that we are not led to accept or support in any way any organization, cause or measure which, in its remotest effect, would jeopardize free agency, whether it be in politics, government, religion, employment, education, or any other field. *It is not enough for us to be sincere in what we support. We must be right!*[5] (Emphasis added.)

The Prophet Nephi declares that the devil's great evil organization would hold dominion throughout every nation in the world and that, except for a very few who are true to the Church of the Lamb of God, all others by default belong to that enormous evil organization:

> And it came to pass that the angel spake unto me, Nephi, saying: . . . Look, and behold that great and abominable church, which is the mother of abominations, whose founder is the devil.

> And he said unto me: Behold there are save two churches only; the one is the church of the Lamb of God, and the other is the church of the devil; wherefore, whoso belongeth not to the church of the Lamb of God belongeth to that great church, which is the mother of abominations; and she is the whore of all the earth.
>
> And it came to pass that I looked and beheld the whore of all the earth, and she sat upon many waters; and she had dominion over all the earth, among all nations, kindreds, tongues, and people. . . .
>
> And it came to pass that I beheld that the great mother of abominations did gather together multitudes upon the face of all the earth, among all the nations of the Gentiles, to fight against the Lamb of God (1 Nephi 14:5, 9-11, 13).

It can be clearly seen then in this prophecy that:

1. Satan's "most abominable" church will have great dominion, power and authority among all nations of the earth in these days.

2. All those who do not belong to Jesus Christ's Church will belong to the church of the devil.

3. This great "whore of all the earth" will eventually "gather together multitudes upon the face of all the earth, among all nations of the Gentiles, to fight against [the Saints of] the Lamb of God" (See 1 Nephi 13:5, Daniel 7:21, 7:25, Revelation 13:7).

Ezra Taft Benson frequently expressed his opinion that the ultimate nature of this war will be a fight for the agency of man:

> It was the struggle over free agency that divided us before we came here; [and] it may well be the struggle over the same principle which will deceive and divide us again.[6]

Satan's Church is prophesied to arise in the latter-days and wield a massive amount of power and "dominion over all the earth" (1 Nephi 14:9-11). Latter-day Saints should be concerned about the workings of Satan's church, as there will come a time when persecution by this satanic organization will become almost unbearable and will "wear out the saints of the Most High" (Daniel 7:21, 25; Revelation 13:7).

In order to have a better understanding of how this may come to pass, a number of current organizations whose unabashed goals are to control the world and subvert all religions into a one worldwide religious body will be discussed.

The information that will follow shows that New Age organizations are a major arm of Satan's great last days outreach. The New Age movement's stated goals match many of Satan's goals, and this is not by coincidence. At its basic levels, the New Age movement is merely a revival of ancient mysticism and occult practices, updated to appeal to modern tastes.

The more one learns about the New Age, the more prepared he is to resist its already far-reaching influences. The scriptures show that the Lord has continually warned against evils that are major tenants of the New Age movement. This book puts faces and names on many organizations and practices the Lord has warned about. Let there be no doubt: the New Age movement openly strives to destroy Christianity and set up a world religion and government. Your worship and freedoms are at stake.

Although Satan will eventually lose his ability to influence men, Elder Bruce R. McConkie describes the success Satan will have before he is bound. It will be "an evil day, a damnable day" and darkness will cover the earth:

> Of the evil and iniquity destined to cover the earth before the Second Coming, the apostle Paul said: "The mystery of iniquity doth already work—it has even now commenced—and he [Lucifer] it is who now worketh, and Christ suffereth him to work"—it is part of the plan that men be tempted of the devil—until the time is fulfilled that he shall be taken out of the way." That is, Satan shall go to and fro upon the earth, raging in the hearts of men, until he is bound in the millennial day. . . . (JST, 2 Thessalonians 2:1-9).
>
> . . . He and his works have been manifest in all ages. And the worst lies ahead. . . . When darkness covers the earth and

apostasy is everywhere, then sin and evil rear their ugly heads over all the earth and are everywhere to be found. And the darker the apostate night, the more evil and damning are the sins. . . . Jesus, in speaking of the day in which there would be a falling away from his gospel, said: "Iniquity shall abound" (JS-M 1:30). It could not be otherwise in such an age. Sin and every evil thing always abound when there is apostasy. Their presence today is one of the signs of the times. Without God and true religion in their lives, men sink into unbelievable depths of degradation.[7]

Chapter Two

WHAT IS THE NEW AGE MOVEMENT?

Many Americans have never heard of the New Age movement yet they already accept and believe in many of its practices and teachings. "New Age" ideas are becoming increasingly popular throughout the world. They embrace trance channeling, crystal healing, reincarnation, spirit guides, spirit mediums or channelers, ESP, crystals, Karma, out of body travel, the ancient practices and beliefs of occultism, mind sciences, Eastern mysticism, metaphysics and many others. The New Age movement emphasizes the paranormal, the harnessing of specific mental powers and procedures to draw energy from crystals, as well as "channeled" messages and instructions from the dead.

Many of the roots and beliefs of the modern New Age Movement can be traced back to occultist and medium Helena Petrovna Blavatsky. She was born August 12, 1831 in Russia. She purportedly communed and had face-to-face meetings with so-called ascended masters who instructed her to organize the Theosophical Society. She believed these spirit guides ("Ascended Masters of Wisdom") are highly evolved souls who have gone through numerous reincarnations and are now guiding mankind with their enlightened, superior wisdom. They allegedly dictated to her many of the beliefs found in her major works; *Isis Unveiled* and *The Secret Doctrine*. These writings of Blavatsky laid the early groundwork for modern New Age beliefs and doctrines. It should come as no surprise that these teachings, which blend Eastern and

Western religious sources, are in direct opposition to those of Jesus Christ.

The "Plan" to Overthrow Christianity

The New Age Movement has a master plan to overthrow Christianity and all other religions that refuse to worship Lucifer. It is called, simply, *"THE PLAN."*[8] This great Luciferian Conspiracy was outlined in the 18th century by Adam Weishaupt and Helena Blavatsky, and later was improved and refined by Alice Bailey. When Alice Bailey died in 1949 she had outlined in her book, *Externalization of the Hierarchy*, a step-by-step plan to destroy Christianity and all others who would not adhere to the concepts of the New Age Movement.[9]

New Age researcher Gary Kah, in his exposé of the New Age movement and some of its leaders, explains:

> . . . The work of Alice Bailey is probably the most important in laying the foundation of the New Age movement. By the time she had finished her work in 1949, she had established Lucis Trust, World Goodwill, Triangles, the Arcane School, and the New Group of World Servers; she had written twenty-four books, a total of 10,469 pages, most of which were allegedly written through her by her spirit guide, The Tibetan, Djwhal Khul. . . .
>
> . . . Lucis Trust, an organization which Bailey originally founded in the 1920s under the name Lucifer Publishing Company, today boasts a membership of approximately six thousand people. Some of the world's most renowned financial and political leaders have belonged to this organization; including individuals such as Robert McNamara, Donald Regan, Henry Kissinger, David Rockefeller, Paul Volker, and George Schultz. This is the same group of people that runs the Council on Foreign Relations, the organization responsible for founding the United Nations. It is interesting to note that Lucis Trust was headquartered at United Nations Plaza until recently.

... Alice began a metamorphosis which transformed her into a master teacher of the occult and one of the most receptive channels of demonic influence the world had yet known.[10]

It may be helpful at this point to review some of the perverse New Age religious doctrines, imitations, counterfeits, and practices that have been instituted by Satan and embraced by various levels of the New Age organizations. Note that the doctrines and practices of the New-Age World Religion mirror those of ancient Babylonian society. Following is a partial list of some of their doctrinal beliefs, customs and mind-expanding programs, although not all are presented in the flattering terminology preferred by adherents:

New Age/Occult Practices

altered states of consciousness
ancient practices of occultism
astral travel
astrology
automatic writing
bio-feedback
channeled messages from the dead
contact with the dead
corporeal possession
crystal healing
decrees
divination
drug and alcohol abuse
eastern mysticism
emphasis on the paranormal
ESP
evolution doctrine
experiential religion
fire worship
goddess worship
hypnotism
karma
levitation
magic words (mantras)
metaphysics
mind sciences
mystic teachings and initiations
nature/earth worship
necromancy
no-touch therapy
numerology
occultisms
occult meditation
occult symbolism
Ouija boards
out-of-body travel
palmistry
psychedelic New Age music
psychic mind powers
rebirthing or reincarnation
rolfing
seances
scientific-spiritualism
self-love
sexual licentiousness
shamanism
Silva Mind Control
spirit guides
spirit mediums
trance channeling
UFO manifestations
visualization
walk-ins (possession)

Satanic Spirits Inspire New Age Thought

The New Age movement of today embraces, promotes and looks for direction from these same demon-inspired teachings. They make contact with these demonic entities through a variety of ways, the majority of which put a person's mind in an altered state of consciousness. They use visualization, meditation, music, color therapy, incense, gemology, sexual ritual, drug ingestion, Yoga, automatic writing and channeling of spirits to achieve deeper levels of relaxation and ease communication with these so-called enlightened spiritual sources.

A great many of the New Age leaders have openly admitted that these supernatural spirit teachers were the source of their inspiration. For an example we have Alice Bailey, through whom the Tibetan master Djwhal Khul dictated twenty-five books; "Seth," who channels through Jan Roberts; Ruth Montgomery, who has admitted having many spirit guides that inspire her writing. There is Tuella, who is the channel for the Ashtar Command; and a number of advanced spiritual personages who claim to be representatives of a Intergalactic Space Confederation who are waiting in the wings to save a selected portion of humanity from the catastrophic events they say are coming upon mankind. There is Ramtha, a purported enlightened 35,000-year-old "Lemurian" who claims to be a warrior-king who conquered Atlantis. Ex-housewife J. Z. Knight allows him to take over her body and speak as a trance channel.

New Age leaders, along with their enlightened spirit guides, teach the doctrine of selfism. They teach that man is the only god; there is no other. They accept Jesus as a great teacher but reject all claims of his divinity as the son of God. In their view, Jesus Christ is no more God than anyone else is. The New Age believes that Jesus became "the Christ" only after he purified himself of "bad karma" by going through numerous incarnations. In their view he is only one of many "masters" who assist humanity from a superior (although not the highest) plane of existence.

There is an increasing appeal in New Age circles toward the pagan belief in an "earth mother" deity, as opposed to a heavenly

Father. They deny the sacrifice and atonement of Jesus on the cross. As New Age Prophetess Elizabeth Clare Prophet explains:

> . . . the erroneous doctrine concerning the blood sacrifice of Jesus—which he himself never taught—has been perpetuated to the present hour, a remnant of pagan rite long refuted by the Word of God. God the Father did not require the sacrifice of his son Christ Jesus, or of any other incarnation for the sins of the world . . . .[11]

New Age ideology is based upon astrologically defined beliefs rather than those that are biblically defined. Thus the New Age is thoroughly occultic and completely unchristian.

The "Aquarian Conspiracy"

Ardent New Age guru and prophetess Marilyn Ferguson proudly describes the New Age Movement as the "*Aquarian Conspiracy.*" She states:

> The Aquarian Conspirators range across all levels of income and education, from the humblest to the highest. There are schoolteachers and office workers, famous scientists, government officials and lawmakers, artists and millionaires, taxi drivers and celebrities, leaders in medicine, education, law, psychology. Some are open in their advocacy, and their names may be familiar. . . .
>
> There are legions of conspirators. They are in corporations, universities and hospitals, on the faculties of public schools, in factories and doctors' offices, in state and federal agencies, on city councils and the White House staff, in state legislatures, in volunteer organizations, in virtually all arenas of policy-making in the country.[12]

Peter Lalonde, Christian editor of the *Omega Letter*, pointed out some problems which New Age followers had to overcome in order to entice and deceive a greater number of Americans into accepting New Age teachings and practices:

> The obvious stumbling block to this "world-wide revival of Shamanism" was of course, materialistic, scientific, Christian America....
>
> However, as we have seen with the rise of the New Age Movement, all that was needed to gain a foothold in this great land was a change of terminologies... not practices.
>
> Thus, what was once called a demon is now called a "spirit guide" and what was once called a seance is now called a trance-channeling session.
>
> You see, Christian America would never accept Satanism but... when it comes in the name of the latest medical science, or the newest discovery of physics, or the most successful business seminar, America is receiving it with open arms....
>
> As one New Age leader put it: "One of the biggest advantages we have as New Agers is, once the occult, metaphysical and New Age terminology is removed, we have concepts and techniques that are very acceptable to the general public. So we can change the names and demonstrate the power. In so doing, we open the New Age door to millions who normally would not be receptive."
>
> You see, nothing has changed. Only the names are different. And millions are being deceived by this "wolf in sheep's clothing."[13]

The Lord has counseled the Saints to beware of false prophets who come in sheep's clothing but inwardly are ravening wolves. He taught that by their fruits ye shall know them (see Matthew 7: 13-20; 3 Nephi 14:13-20).

Elder Orson Pratt noted the long-term success Satan has had in giving old satanic practices new names:

> The devil has invented various names for his manifestations in order to get the people to swallow them down; the same as the doctors. When they wish to administer some nauseous kind of medicine, they sweeten it up a little. So the devil has sweetened up these things in such a way that he has got almost all

these manifestations under the name of science. If you want to see a species of devilism made manifest, it comes out under a scientific phraseology, under the specious name of electro-biology, animal-magnetism, or some such popular name—names that have been given to real sciences, which have their laws, founded in nature, are now given to these supernatural manifestations. Why does Satan use these artifices? Because the people at the present day have become naturally scientific, or a great many of them have; and the devil thinks if he can only invent a real, nice, beautiful name, with some resemblance to a scientific name, a great many of these persons will swallow it down, and think it all right.[14]

The alarming fact is that he has been succeeding to a appalling degree with his trickery even among the Saints.

Rejection of Jesus Christ Is a New Age Doctrine

The New Age Movement is the spiritual form for One Worldism. It is critically important that this spiritual "adhesive" be in place before this One Worldism or "One World Order" can be attained. A spiritual system needs human agents through which these enlightened mystical forces can work. They, in turn, pass this so-called enlightenment on to others who are searching for some sort of guidance by mystical means from beyond. "The Plan" is coming together:

> The heart of the [New Age] Movement is not about crystals, trance channelers, holistic healers, or reincarnationists, although they are all a part of it. It is not even primarily about the rapidly spreading teachings of "human potential" and the belief that we are gods, although these are also becoming central New Age tenets. Instead, the heart of the New Age movement is the *rejection of hope in Jesus Christ* in the face of these planet-threatening crises. The determination to solve man's problems without God forms the basis of this new humanism called the New Age movement.[15]

This "Human Potential Movement" teaches self-expectance, self-image, self-control, self-esteem, self-motivation, self-awareness, self-direction, self-discipline, self-dimension and self-projection. It teaches that Man is God and there is no other. Man is his own supreme being.[16]

Former New Ager Elliot Miller points out how these beliefs and all that the New Age stands for is in stark opposition to the teachings of Jesus Christ:

> The New Age Movement is *most* significantly a sophisticated, contemporary representation of the same old spiritual kingdom that has always stood in stark opposition to the kingdom of Jesus Christ (for example, Acts 13:8-12).
>
> This fact is wearisomely demonstrated by the spiritual "entities" who through human "channels" supply much of the movement's teaching. They unfailingly make a point of attacking the unique deity of Christ, the atoning power of his death, and so on.
>
> New Agers desperately need this biblical perspective, lest they devote their lives to saving the world, *only to find at the end they were serving the author of its destruction.*[17] (John 8:44; 10:10. Emphasis added.)

Constance Cumbey, in her book *The Hidden Dangers Of The Rainbow,* states:

> The glue binding most New Age devotees is one of common mystical experiences. "Experiential religion" is considered vital within the Movement. A substantial proportion of those within the Movement strongly believe in psychic phenomena and say they do so because of "direct experiences."
>
> Those among their number who have not participated in the communal tripping of the "Light Fantastic" are encouraged to try meditation, LSD, or any one of the scores of "psychotechnologies" promised to induce "transformation"—a euphemism for progressively deeper levels of demonic influence.[18]

New Age researcher Texe Marrs, upon examining the powerful forces of the New Age Movement, has this to say concerning "their evil objectives":

> What I discovered staggers the imagination. The New Age Movement has undeniably taken on the definite form of a religion, complete with an agreed-upon body of doctrine, printed scripture, a pattern of worship and ritual, a functioning group of ministers and lay leaders, and an effective outreach program carried out by an active core proselytizing believers. Furthermore, because of its astonishing success in attracting new followers, the New Age Church now has a large and growing membership worldwide. Its avowed aim, however, is to become the only world religion.[19]

The plans of the New Age Movement include the elimination of several billion people from the earth's population, which they say must be accomplished before the year 2000 if the world is to survive.[20]

Many watchdogs claim the New Age movement has spent millions of dollars training its members and "planting" them in fundamental churches around the United States supposedly to influence the congregations. It doesn't bother these plants to attend Christian churches—the newest form of blasphemy is to praise the Lord and act like a Christian while laughing inside the whole time.

Marrs points out:

> New Age leaders know that only if they are able to undermine credibility in the Bible, discredit Jesus Christ, and weaken the example of Christian churches can they succeed in their ultimate objective: the ascension to power of a New Age Messiah (the Antichrist) and the establishment of a one world order. At the pinnacle of this one world order will be the religious system described in Revelation 17: MYSTERY, BABYLON THE GREAT, THE MOTHER OF HARLOTS AND ABOMINATIONS OF THE EARTH.[21]

Marrs then describes in greater detail this "New Age World Religion":

> The New Age is a universal, open-arms religion that excludes from its ranks only those who believe in Jesus Christ and a personal God. Buddhists, Shintoists, Satanists, Secular Humanists, witches, witch doctors, and shamans—all who reject Christianity are invited to become trusted members of the New Age family. Worshippers of separate faiths and denominations are to be unified in a common purpose: the glorification of man....
>
> The New Age doctrine combines the worst of modern psychology, so called "progressive education," medicine, science, and economics in a dangerous and new formulation perfectly compatible with the abominations of paganism and occultism. New Age professionals claim that this is a "High Religion" more attuned to the needs of "thinking" people than Christianity which they deem outmoded and unsophisticated...
>
> The essence of New Age religious doctrine is that man is neither sinful nor evil, and that Jesus' sacrifice on the cross was meaningless and futile...
>
> Predictably, a religious philosophy that deifies man and is totally void of absolute moral restraints is extremely attractive to those who do not know the Lord Jesus Christ as their personal Savior. In a world rampant with sin and unethical conduct, a world devoid of the *agape* love that is in Jesus Christ, the New Age sadly has become a narcissistic religion that readily finds converts....[22]

Texe Marrs states that "witchcraft is also a growing movement among New Agers, who claim that witchcraft is a legitimate religion which has strong similarities to the Eastern religions."[23]

New Age teachings are bound together by a common and growing interest in the occult. Their goal is to eliminate all traditional religions and establish a World Religion based on New Age/Eastern thought. To create a World Religion that encompasses all other religions a set of scriptures would eventually be needed to establish the universal doctrines. New Ager Vera Alder, in her book *When Humanity Comes Of Age*, outlines the movement's plans:

> The ancient wisdom, as it existed in all old civilizations, will be sifted, pieced together, correlated and synthesized with the findings of modern scientists and the developments in religious fields."[24]

New Ager Lola Davis explains that this will come from a variety of sources, many of which are completely incompatible with Christianity:

> In this century, religious writings previously unavailable have been found or released. Among these are the Dead Sea scrolls; the vast treasures of religious writings found in the Potola in Tibet; Christian writings deleted from the Bible during the 4th century; writings of Teilhard de Chardin; and previously carefully guarded knowledge of the Ancient Wisdom, including the writings of the Tibetan in the Alice Bailey books; writings of mystics from various religions; the Buddhism and Hindu philosophies and practices. . . .
>
> Probably much of this knowledge could be advantageously used in synthesizing the major religions with a World Religion for the New Age.[25]

The writings of various New Agers (Kevin Ryerson, Elizabeth Clare Prophet, J. Finley Cooper, Anne Read and others) indicate that "revelation" from channeling sensitives such as Edgar Cayce will show that Christ has been reincarnated several times and is becoming a more perfect teacher each time. New information concerning his younger years will be taught. It will be said that he traveled to India and Tibet where the masters taught him how to become the promised Messiah.[26] Other channeled "enlightened" spiritual entities like Ramtha, and Lazaris and Seth will reveal similar teachings about this cosmic Christ (*false Christ*) who is going to appear. After this softening-up process has made the world seriously question the divinity of Jesus Christ and his scriptures, the world will be ready for more "new" information.

The New Agers believe that society will soon be ready for the satanically-inspired New Age bible which will covertly or openly teach doctrines of astrology, reincarnation, witchcraft, Satanism, karma, hedonism, and other false teachings. The primary ingredient in its teachings will be the doctrine of selfism: man is God and there is no other.[27] In 2 Timothy 3:2, 4, Paul described this apostate philosophy of self that men will turn to in the last days:

> For men shall be lovers of their own selves, covetous, boasters, proud, blasphemers, disobedient to parents, unthankful, unholy. . .
>
> Traitors, heady, highminded, lovers of pleasures more than lovers of God.

The New Agers have openly admitted that the *mind* sciences are part of the movement. The Movement has gained more acceptance through the use of Transcendental Meditation, Holistic Health Centers, etc.

There can be very little question that many people are today communicating with evil spirits from the spirit world; indeed, entire religions and cultures are based on communication with "familiar spirits." Whether these people have been deceived into believing they are speaking with "higher spirits" or whether they worship Satan outright, millions throughout the world have been in contact with the evil spirits who rebelled against The Father and The Son in premortal councils. The Restored Gospel affirms the existence of these demonic spirits, who have opposed the Restored Church ever since they tried to keep young Joseph from praying to the Father in the grove. These spirits vary their messages as circumstances dictate; some will even claim to be messengers of Jesus Christ if it suits their purposes. But the overall objective of these spirits is clear: to lead people away from and eventually deny the existence of God and His Son, Jesus Christ.

Satan has very cleverly convinced many people that they can trust and be "enlightened" by these deceptive and lying minions of his. At the same time he has persuaded many of the Saints that evil spirit entities do not exist, and thus pose no threat to themselves or mankind.

Some people invite these demonic entities to possess their bodies so that they might give instructions to a larger audience. The majority of the messages from these beings promote and expound on New Age doctrines, many of which were first "revealed" in similar channeling sessions. The doctrines and philosophies they promote are very hostile to Christianity and promote the New Age one-world religion and one-world political and social order that is already forming.

These spiritual contacts are becoming more and more frequent, much more so than in ages past. Our society is gradually being conditioned to be receptive to them and view them as superior, enlightened messengers. This renewed interest in the paranormal takes many forms, including UFO visitations, astrology, spiritualism, star-worship, mind-expansion, witchcraft and other ancient practices of occultism. This great shift in religious and social paradigms has the net effect of preparing the world for the establishment of a great world religious system by whose "sorceries were all nations deceived" (Revelation 18:23).

New Ager John Randolph Price stated that Elena, one of his spiritual messengers from beyond, told him that the "Masters" are working to save mankind. They do this by choosing "suitable subjects" for New Age conversion so they can then help establish the New Age World Order. Elena speaks highly of her kind, glorifying these devils from hell for circulating various New Age doctrines.[28]

New Age practitioners make contact with these evil spirits through various methods that put a person in an altered state of consciousness. These methods include visualization, color therapy, yoga, music, drug ingestion, and meditation.

Satan has deceived New Agers into believing that the unembodied spirits that contact them are helpers, teachers, and great instructors and are therefore good. They call them light bearers, spirit guides, spirits of light, spirit counselors, psychic advisors, ancient masters, masters of wisdom, etc.

New Age Symbols Engulf the World

According to New Age watchdogs, New Age occultists kept their basic symbols and practices secret until 1975 when through demonic instructions they were given permission to go public with their directives to the world.

Since then, a flood of New Age symbols have become commonplace in many aspects of society. These ancient satanic symbols can be seen in television ads, Saturday morning cartoons, movies, music, clothing, games, computer software, and in an increasing number of general books and magazines. Texe Marrs elaborates:

> ... You'll be amazed. We are literally deluged with Satanic symbols—with pentagrams, triangles, rainbows, perverted crosses, pyramids, and more. The images are usually presented to us either in a subtle, indirect way or up front in a positive manner. Rarely are we given the impression that there is anything wrong with these images.[29]

Some others are the hexagram, peace symbol, and unicorns.

Loosely Structured Or Very Organized?

Thousands of loosely-knit organizations today are linked together in a worldwide network. Together they are known as the *New Age Movement*. Their main objectives are the creation of a "New World Order" and a New World Religion. They have successfully penetrated almost every area of our private, religious and professional lives.

Even within the New Age Movement itself there is a wide variety of opinions as to how loosely or tightly it is organized. Is it the result of a carefully masterminded plot by some sinister, conspiratorial insiders? Or is it just a bunch of loose-knit organizations that have found it advantageous to work together for the same idyllic goals?

New Agers fall under both extremes and anywhere in between, depending on how high up in the movement they are. The higher you are in any organization, the more information you will have about its inner workings, goals and future plans. The "foot soldiers" in most organizations, the New Age movement included, are not always privy to this inside information, as they could unknowingly alert the opposition to their plans and activities. It would be ridiculous to assert that millions of New Agers are all in on a plot to destroy Christianity and set up oppressive government and religious practices. Indeed, all but a select few have been deceived, and suppose that they are doing good. Despite their supposed lack of malice, the rank and file of the New Age movement nevertheless help carry out the plans and designs of their leaders. Without having any more than a minimal understanding of the New Age movement's ultimate objectives, millions are proselyting others to the worship of "self," or even worse, to the satanic practices of spiritualism.

Constance Cumbey, in her book *The Hidden Dangers Of The Rainbow*, points out that many virtually-mainstream movements are part of the New Age:

> . . . the so-called Age of Aquarius, encompasses a number of groups and submovements, such as: the Holistic Movement, Humanistic Psychology, Transpersonal Psychology, Humanistic Movement, New Thought, Third Wave, Third Force, The New Spirituality, the Human Potential Movement, Secular Humanism, and Humanism. . . .
>
> Marilyn Ferguson's *The Aquarian Conspiracy*, an important New Age manifesto, attempts to announce and popularize what the New Agers chose to publicly display in their Movement. Heavily extolling the joys of *"altered states of consciousness. . . ."*
>
> Organizations as diverse as Amnesty International, Greenpeace, the Sierra Club, Children of God, and Zero Population Growth openly and proudly bill themselves as "New Age."
>
> The New Agers propose to establish gigantic global agencies such as a World Food Authority, World Water Authority, and an authority to administer a universal draft and universal

tax. They have pointed to such legislative proposals as the Peace Academy as proof of their success in advertising towards the New World Order. They intend to give us a "Universal Credit Card" not to mention a *"New World Religion"* (Emphasis added).

The New Age Movement's deep and abiding hatred for Jews, Catholics, Protestant fundamentalists, and orthodox Moslems in particular, and all Christians in general has been reaffirmed in the numerous David Spangler writings and tapes as well as those of other current New Age leaders. . . .

They have made flat statements in writing that they plan to outlaw the present religious practices and symbols of orthodox Jews and Christians.[30]

They claim that master "messiahs" will appear to adherents of all the present major world religions to persuade them of the "truths" of the New World Religion and its "New Revelation."[31]

New Ager Marilyn Ferguson outlines a conspiracy of *piecemeal and progressive infiltration and takeover* that includes such key areas of influence as the educational institutions, workforce, and therapists' offices. The power to influence receptive minds is at its highest here. As will be seen later, this has, to a large extent, been done.

Former New Age devotee Elliot Miller, in his book *A Crash Course on The New Age Movement*, explains the movement this way:

The New Age movement is best understood as a *network*—or, to be more exact, a metanetwork (network of networks). . . Networks are typically informal, loosely knit organizations which are very different in both structure and operation from other types of organizations:

. . . There are many different levels of networking, so that one network can exist within a larger network, which in turn can exist within a still larger one (that is, a metanetwork).

> ... Within the New Age metanetwork and movement are hundreds of smaller (but still sometimes very large) networks and movements encompassing a wide variety of interests and causes (all compatible with the ends of the larger network). The consciousness movement (that is, those who have advocated developing altered states of consciousness as a means of expanding human possibilities), the holistic health movement, the human potential movement—all have contributed generously to the New Age movement. So have the followers of many Eastern gurus and Western occult and "metaphysical" teachers. However participation in such movements as holistic health or human potential does not always indicate conscious or actual participation in the NAM (remember that networks have fuzzy borderlines). Nor do all Eastern or metaphysical movements believe in a coming new age; neither do they all participate in the networking process.
>
> ... *The New Age movement then is an extremely large, loosely structured network of organizations and individuals bound together by common values (based in mysticism and monism—the world view that "all is one") and a common vision (a coming "new age" of peace and mass enlightenment, the "Age of Aquarius").*[32] (Emphasis added.)

Notice the striking similarities between Elliot Miller's description of the New Age movement and the definition of the ancient meaning of the term *great and abominable church* in the January Ensign in 1988 by Stephen E. Robinson, an associate professor of ancient scripture at Brigham Young University:

> The word great in the phrase great and abominable church is an adjective of size rather than quality and ... [it] informs us of the great size of the abominable entity ...
>
> The term *abominable* is used in the Old Testament to describe what God hates, what cannot fail to arouse his wrath.
>
> The word *church* had a slightly broader meaning anciently than it does now. *It referred to an assembly, congregation, or association of people who bonded together and shared the same*

loyalties. Thus, the term was not necessarily restricted to religious associations . . .

When we put this together, we find that the term great and abominable church means an immense assembly or association of people bound together by their loyalty to that which God hates . . . [33] (Emphasis Added.)

As has been be shown, the ancient meaning of the term *great and abominable* quite closely represents the tenants of the organization collectively known as the "New Age Movement." It is not suggested that the New Age movement and the great and abominable church of the devil spoken of in the scriptures are one and the same entity, but merely that many of the identifying characteristics of both are similar and thus worth our attention. Both represent the false beliefs and ideologies of Satan and embrace mysteries and unspeakable practices that are an abomination to the Lord.

The New Age movement is larger, more sophisticated, diverse and out in the open about many of its goals and objectives than ever before. But even with all its window dressing, it is still the same old satanic spiritual power that has always been an enemy of all Holiness (See Acts 13:4-23). The very name Satan means "opposition" and "enemy of righteousness."[34] This fact is clearly evident when channeled spirit entities who dictate much of the New Age's timetables and agenda consistently oppose Jesus Christ, his atonement and his resurrection.

Many New Agers use mind altering "psychotechnologies" of chanting, "creative visualization," meditation, and drugs to reach the ultimate mystical experience of the mind. These consciousness-altering techniques can bring their thought patterns to a stop without extinguishing or diminishing consciousness itself. In this self-induced state they are opened to "spiritual" contacts and enlightenment. Naturally, after such mind-blowing experiences they are inclined to believe they understand reality while everyone else is confused and unenlightened.[35] Perhaps it is of this type of person that the Lord declares in Isaiah 66:4: "I also will choose their delusions, and will bring their fears upon them; because when I called, none did answer; when I spake, they did not hear: but they did evil before mine eyes, and chose [that] in which I delighted not."

Paul explains that in our day Satan will come with all power, signs, lying wonders and deceptions, sending many strong delusions, that they should believe a lie and be damned; *because "they believed not the truth, but had pleasure in unrighteousness"* (See 2 Thessalonians 2:9-12).

Since New Agers' information comes through "enlightened" spiritual guidance counselors or hypnosis and regression to another life, others have no way of knowing whether their experiences are figments of their imagination, actual spirit contact, or a combination of both. How can a person being deceived know the reality of what he is experiencing? How can they see that it is they who are confused and unenlightened and suffering from strong delusions of the mind? Yet they hope to blend mysticism and unverifiable psychic experiences with objective science.[36] As New Age thinking and influence permeate the scientific community, scientific objectivity may be lost.

New Age Christian researcher Peter Lalonde explains:

> Years ago students of Bible prophecy who watched the world scene for signs of the prophesied New World Order had a much easier time of it. All they had to do was observe a few key organizations such as the United Nations, the Aspen Institute, the Council on Foreign Relations, or the Trilateral Commission and see what plans they were espousing to build a world community. Their lofty plans and goals were seen as a foreshadow of the prophetic events we knew would one day come to pass.
>
> However, the emergence of the New Age movement and the thousands of different groups working toward this New World Order has made the task of discerning the true centers of global power much more difficult. This increasing difficulty has to do not only with the vastly increasing number of groups but also with the fact that many of the groups working toward this

New World Order do not appear on the surface to be doing so at all.[37]

Gary Kah says he has discovered that most hard core New Age organizations belong to other, more powerful organizations. It became evident to him that within the large network of organizations, a common mindset exists in which they collaborate to bring about certain end results—the ushering in of a New Age:

> The inner circle of the New Age movement (in Western society) seems to consist of individuals from the highest levels of Freemasonry, along with important members of other slightly less powerful "policy making" groups such as the Club of Rome, the Council on Foreign Relations, and the Trilateral Commission (whose leaders are often closely connected with, or are themselves members of, the Masonic Institution). These so-called round-table groups are closely tied to the United Nations and receive much of their funding from various international financiers who are also part of the Masonic network. (According to the *World Book Encyclopedia*—1986 Edition, more than one hundred organizations maintain a special relationship with Freemasonry.)
> Lucis Trust and its immediate network of organizations, on the other hand, seem to be the main link between the secret societies of Freemasonry and the public, serving as a type of "go between." Their purpose, as I see it, has been to prepare the way for the New World Order, by conditioning the masses to accept its "spiritual" principles. (It only makes sense. If a world government was ever to take place, it would have to go public at some point; it could not be kept secret forever.) The process of conditioning society has been going on for about one hundred years, but it has greatly intensified during the last generation. . . .[38]

Many who belong to this wide-spread movement have simply been deceived, and do not know the ultimate objectives of its leaders. However, even at its lower levels, the movement declares an utter contempt for Christianity, the traditional family, and many basic moral values. Its propaganda is wide-spread and can be found in television shows, movies, music, political forums, and most importantly, in your own school district's classrooms.

Both the Book of Revelation and New Age gurus agree that in the last days there will be a great push to convince the world that a great savior has come to deliver the world from all its ills. Both agree that this "savior" *will not* be the Lord Jesus Christ. Much of the world will herald the coming of this anti-Christ. New Age followers are working diligently (albeit subtly) to prepare the world to welcome this false savior. Latter-day Saints will need the gift of the Holy Ghost to detect this and other false messiahs (Matthew 24: 23-24), for great will be their influence and power over the children of men. So convincing and appealing will these anti-Christs be that many, including those belonging to the Lord's kingdom, will be deceived.

President Ezra Taft Benson confirmed ancient Book of Mormon prophecies that secret combinations would thrive and increase their evil influence throughout the world in our day (see 2 Nephi 26: 20-22):

> Wickedness is rapidly expanding in every segment of our society (see D & C 1:14-16; 84:49-53). It is more highly organized, more cleverly disguised, and more powerfully promoted than ever before. Secret combinations lusting for power, gain, and glory are *flourishing*. A secret combination that seeks to overthrow the freedom of all lands, nations, and countries is increasing its evil influence and control over America and the entire world (see Ether 8:18-25).[39]

The Saints will be tried, tested and proven in their resolve, commitment and loyalty to the Savior before his Second Coming, when all the righteous will be saved. They can best be prepared if they have a knowledge of both God's plans and Satan's plans. It cannot be forgotten that Satan is very real and his mission is to deceive. Those Saints who think a "conspiracy scenario" sounds far-fetched, would do well to remember these warnings from the Lord:

And now I show unto you a mystery, a thing which is had in secret chambers, to bring to pass even your destruction in process of time, and ye knew it not (D & C 38:13);

Also from the Doctrine and Covenants,

And again, I say unto you that the enemy in the secret chambers seeketh your lives, . . . but ye know not the hearts of men in your own land (D & C 38:28-29).

And from the Book of Mormon,

Wherefore, O ye Gentiles, it is wisdom in God that these things should be shown unto you, that thereby ye may repent of your sins, and suffer not that these murderous combinations shall get above you, which are built up to get power and gain— and the work, yea, even the work of destruction come upon you, yea, even the sword of the justice of the Eternal God shall fall upon you, to your overthrow and destruction if ye shall suffer these things to be (Ether 8:23).

The Lord has said that it would be wise to learn of the great, murderous combinations that will come among the Saints during the latter days, in order to combat them. Our leaders have also warned that any organization that would take away our agency is of the devil. It is our responsibility to identify organizations that would restrict or destroy our God-given freedoms.

Latter-day Saints Need To Become Informed

As members of the true Church of the Lord, Latter-day Saints should be aware of these plans and watch as the time nears that they will be implemented so as to not be deceived by them when their implementation takes place. Armed with this knowledge of the plans of the New Age Movement, the warning in the scriptures to members of the church or those of *"the covenant"* becomes much clearer. "For false Christs, and false prophets shall rise, and shall shew signs and wonders, to seduce, if it were possible, even the elect (Mark 13:22).

Explaining our responsibilities, President Marion G. Romney said:

> I am persuaded that if we are to 'conquer Satan, and . . . escape the hands of the servants of Satan [that] do uphold his work' (D & C 10:5), we must understand and recognize the situation as it is. This is no time for us to bury our heads in the sand, to equivocate or panic. The difficulties of our times have not caught us unawares. . . . We know that as the second coming of the Savior approaches, the tempo of Satan's campaign for the souls of men is being, and will continue to be, accelerated. . . .
>
> We know that the Spirit of Christ and the power of his priesthood is ample shield to the power of Satan. We know that there is available to each of us the gift of the Holy Ghost—the power of revelation—which embraces the gift of discernment by which we may unerringly detect the devil and the counterfeits he is so successfully foisting upon this gullible generation.[40]

Chapter Three

"THE PLAN"—
THE NEW WORLD RELIGION

In his book *Dark Secrets of the New Age*, Texe Marrs outlines the thirteen-point Master Plan, referred to as "The Plan," which Satan has concocted in order to bring this prophesied anti-god religious system of world domination into reality in the last days:

Point #1
The principle aim of The Plan is to establish a One World, New Age Religion and a one world political and social order.

Point #2
The New Age World Religion will be a revival of the idolatrous religion of ancient Babylon in which mystery cults, sorcery and occultism, and immorality flourished.

Point #3
The Plan is to come to fullness when the New Age Messiah, the Antichrist with the number 666, comes in the flesh to lead the unified New Age World Religion and oversee the new one world order.

Point #4
Spirit guides (demons) will help man inaugurate the New Age and will pave the way for the Antichrist, the New Age mangod, to be acclaimed by humanity as the Great World Teacher.

Point #5
"World Peace," "Love!" and "Unity!" will be the rallying cries of the New Age World Religion.

Point #6
New Age teachings are to be taught and propagated in every sphere of society around the globe.

Point #7
New Age leaders and believers will spread the apostasy that Jesus is neither God nor the Christ.

Point #8
Christianity and all other religions are to become integral parts of the New Age World Religion.

Point #9
Christian principles must be discredited and abandoned.

Point #10
Children will be spiritually seduced and indoctrinated and the classroom used to promote New Age dogma.

Point #11
Flattery will be employed to entice the world into believing that man is a divine god.

Point #12
Science and the New Age World Religion will become one.

Point #13
Christians who resist The Plan will be dealt with. If necessary, they will be exterminated and the world "purified."[41]

In the March 1991 *Ensign*, R. Kim Davis explains how New Age spiritual beliefs are opposed to Christ and his teachings and how the saints should rely on the Holy Ghost to avoid its pitfalls. He explains the New Age Movement as:

> . . . an eclectic, contemporary pseudo-religion that consists of a confusing array of beliefs about the nature of man and

denies the existence of a personal God and the need for a Savior.

Some aspects of the New Age movement may seem harmless. But when we compare basic principles of the gospel with New Age philosophies, we see that New Age beliefs can lead us away from our Heavenly Father, allowing us to rationalize behavior and become ensnared in sin.

1. A fundamental principle of the gospel is that we are literally the spirit children of a loving heavenly Father, created in his image. We have individual identities and the potential to become like God. (See Genesis 1:26-27; Romans 8:16; Ephesians 4:6; Moses 3:5)

In contrast, the New Age movement defines God as the ultimate reality, a source of pure undifferentiated energy, consciousness, or life-force. Humanity is considered an extension of God, the divine essence that is humanity's higher self. Such a view denies a personal God.

2. Another fundamental principle of the gospel is that we can return to our Father in Heaven through the atonement of Jesus Christ. We know that the separation of man from God began with the fall of Adam and continues as a consequence of sin. Through the atonement and our obedience to the laws and ordinances of the gospel, we can overcome this separation and gain eternal life. (See 1 Corinthians 15:21-22; Mosiah 3:19)

The New Age movement holds that sin does not separate man from God, but that metaphysical ignorance separates us from higher consciousness. New Age beliefs hold that the fall of man is not due to Adam's transgression and its effect on mankind, but is due to mankind's inability to understand the unity of reality. The destiny of man is to achieve somehow a level in which individual consciousness dissolves into the consciousness of the cosmos. Of course, such a philosophy denies individual worth and the need for a Savior.[42]

One of the main tenets of Hinduism is the belief that the spirit is subject to an indefinite series of existences through reincarnation. Most New Agers also believe in the ancient Hindu doctrines of reincarnation and karma. These doctrines state that whatever a person does returns to him and that since people don't have time to experience all the karma in one life, they have to reincarnate in other forms or lives until the good and bad karma are balanced. Elder Bruce R. McConkie explains:

> Reincarnation or the transmigration of souls—the rebirth of the same spirits in new bodily forms in successive ages—is a false doctrine originating with the devil (Teachings, pp. 104-105). It runs counter to the whole system and plan of salvation whereunder spirits are born in pre-existence are permitted to pass through a mortal probation, and then in due course become immortal, incorruptible, and eternal in nature. It is appointed unto man once to be born, "once to die" (Hebrews 9:27), once to be resurrected, and thereafter to "die no more" (Alma 11:45; 12:18; D & C 63:49).[43]

Davis goes on to explain the other two major doctrinal points of difference:

> **3.** We know that God has always revealed his will through prophets on the earth who act as his spokesmen. We also know that we can pray directly to God for personal revelation. (See Amos 3:7; James 1:5; Jacob 4:4; 3 Nephi 18:19-20; D & C 1:37-38; D & C 112:10).
>
> In contrast, New Age approaches to communication with the supernatural may include chanting, ritual, drugs, music, guides—anything that will assist the mind to reach a New Age metaphysical state. New Age philosophy thus denies the fundamental gospel principles concerning man's communication with God.
>
> **4.** We know that the true Church of Jesus Christ was restored to earth so that we need not be tossed to and fro by every wind of doctrine. We can distinguish truth from error. Heavenly Father provides the plan by which his kingdom on earth is administered. (See Ephesians 4:11-14; D & C 20).

The New Age movement tries to replace the commandments of God and the consequences of sin with an experiential view of life in which any type of behavior is potentially acceptable. New Age philosophy suggests that if everything is God, everything is permissible.

The truth is, oneness with our Father in Heaven is made possible only by keeping his commandments. We can achieve peace in this life not by losing our identities in becoming part of the cosmos, but by comprehending our true identities as spirit children of Heavenly Father and personally receiving our Savior.

There should be no doubt that the basic tenets of the New Age movement are directly opposed to the teachings of Jesus Christ and His church. We can avoid the pitfalls of this and other trends that oppose our Savior by relying on the Holy Ghost to help us discern carefully between truth and falsehood.[44] (Emphasis added.)

Some Christians View LDS with Hostility

Latter-day Saints have been placed at a disadvantage by other Christians who have been deceived into believing that the Saints are not allied with them in the fight against the New Age occult practices. Books and videos by purported Christian authors depict our Church as a demonic cult which does not believe in Jesus Christ as our Savior and that our teachings parallel those of the demonic New Age culture; this pits them against us also, as well as the New Agers. They recommend to their Christian readership that they avoid the Latter-day Saint religion/organization and lump it with The Temple of Set, Church of Wicca, Transcendental Meditation and others of the New Age camp.

A well-publicized example of the growing hostilities and misunderstandings about the Latter-day Saints was released by the Associated Press in late June, 1994. The executive director of a evangelical Christian homeless shelter in Albuquerque rejected an offer of help from an LDS group that asked to help serve meals at the rescue mission. The reason given was *"a major doctrinal gulf"* that the director said existed between Mormonism and his vein of Christianity. He said he was impelled to draw the line because the differences in the doctrines of Mormonism and what he considered to be the true gospel. He claimed that even though "Mormons, Jehovah's Witnesses, Scientologists, and followers of Sun Yung Moon's Unification Church claim to be Christians," he believes their views are incompatible with biblical Christianity.

It may be that as this gigantic "Aquarian Conspiracy" continues to grow and polarize the New Age forces from those who will not join their movement, the Latter-day Saint community will become increasingly isolated and be considered the enemy by both sides. Should the Saints become caught in this type of crossfire, one can only imagine the suffering, persecution and trials they may have yet to go through in defense of their beliefs. It must be realized that a time may come in which the members of the Church will be forced to make an open commitment for or against the Lord Jesus Christ.

Many New Age writings claim that there will be an "initiation" which will be the heart and core of the New World Religion. New Age author David Spangler has defined that initiation as a Luciferic initiation. Those who cannot accept the "New Christ" *will be sent to another dimension other than physical incarnation*, he said.[45]

The writings of New Age leaders David Spangler, Moria Timms, Corinne Heline and many others have openly threatened Jews, Christians and Moslems. These New Age leaders believe that those who believe in a personal God and refuse to affiliate with their New World Leader and New World Religion are an inferior species. They speak about sending those that are unfit to another dimension. There will be no place for ignorant people in their "Age of Enlightenment." Those who are not attuned to the spirit of the New Age will not survive. Texe Marrs points out that New Age leaders believe a cleansing will take place that will wipe those Christians from the earth who are unfit to be a part of the New Age, One World lifestyle:

> New Age leaders say that if the coming period of world crises and purification results in suffering and death for unbe-

lievers, so be it—their karma is being worked out. In other words, Christians, Jews, and other unbelievers *deserve exactly what they're getting*. Indeed, it is suggested that pain and suffering are unavoidable. They are part of universal law and serve as preparation for eventual Godhood.[46]

John Randolph Price, a New Age author, outlines in his book *Practical Spirituality* the need for the eradication of two billion people who, as he explains, have lower "vibratory rates."[47] As can be seen, the reality of the New Age propaganda is a far cry from their proposed harmony and enlightenment of the masses but rather the opposite—death, destruction and the annihilation of all who would resist and oppose these satanic plans.

President Brigham Young explained that the scriptures speak of Satan marshaling his forces of deception and waging war against the saints (*See Daniel 7:21-22, Revelation 13:7, 1 Nephi 14:13*). He reiterated many times that the peace that is currently enjoyed is only temporary.[48] Elder Bruce R. McConkie states, ". . . The vision of the future is not all sweetness and light and peace. All that is yet to be shall go forward in the midst of greater evils and perils and desolations than have been known on earth at any time. . . . We have not been promised that the trials and evils of the world will entirely pass us by."[49] The Saints have been warned that in the future they will face conflict, hostility and persecution as Satan organizes his forces against God's kingdom. But he will not prevail.

Chapter Four

THE EXISTENCE OF SATAN AND HIS SPIRIT FOLLOWERS

Priesthood leaders have frequently warned about Satan's ever-expanding attempts to deceive the Saints into participating in evil practices. Elder James E. Faust addressed practices prevalent in the New Age indirectly when he declared that "the mischief of devil worship, sorcery, casting spells, witchcraft, voodooism, black magic, and all other forms of demonism should be avoided like the plague."[50] However, as President Brigham Young has explained, it is also our duty to study and have a knowledge of "evil, and its consequences."[51]

The scriptures declare that willful participation in any of the "spiritual arts," which simply counterfeit the true gifts exercised only by ordained prophets of God, is a sin and "abomination unto the Lord" (Deuteronomy 18:9-14).[52] Enchantments, spells of the wizard, mediums and the necromancer are characteristics of false religions and the superstitions of the world. Those who follow the Holy Ghost and have faith in Jesus Christ will have nothing to do with any form of divination, spirit mediums and spiritual wizardry.

Some within the church seem to see nothing wrong with dabbling in astrology, or talking to a medium or participating in other supernatural experiences. Because they were "told the truth" or saw "parallels" with the restored gospel, they mistakenly believe that there is something good in New Age spiritualism. Bruce R. McConkie explains how this is part of Satan's plan:

> Lucifer is the Great Imitator. He patterns his kingdom after that of God the Lord. The Lord proclaims a plan of salvation; Satan sponsors a plan of damnation. Signs follow those who believe and obey the law of the gospel, and false signs, false wonders, false miracles attend the ministry of the Master of Sin. Knowledge is power, and because he knows more about many things than mortal men, the Great Imitator is able to blind the eyes and deceive the hearts of men and to put his own seal of verity, that of false miracles, on his damning philosophies. Thus those who place themselves wholly at his disposal have power to imitate the deeds of the prophets, as the magicians of Egypt imitated the miracles of Moses and as Simon the sorcerer sought to duplicate the works of Peter.[53]

A Conversation with Lucifer

Samuel H. Roundy, a member of the Church who lived in Salt Lake City in the early part of this century, relates an interesting dream wherein he had a conversation with Lucifer. In that experience Lucifer admitted his continuing desire to deceive the Saints by imitating the works of God through spiritualism and mediumism. While the dream's nature is unknown and is not binding doctrine on the Church, it nevertheless illustrates how Satan's purpose is to deceive the Saints and destroy the work of the Savior:

> In the year 1925 about February 15th, I found myself one night sitting on one side of a table in my home and Lucifer sitting on the other side. How he came I saw not. I immediately asked this question:
> *Roundy: Lucifer why do you seek to destroy and tear down the good works of the Saviour?*
> Lucifer: That is my mission. . . . It was then just like two political parties now. The party that is defeated still thinks its' platform the best. I not only think my plan is the best, but I claim Jesus stole my crown and I am doing all I can to over-

throw his work. We have one very important advantage over the Saints.

Roundy: I asked in what way?

Lucifer: Just think a moment, said he.

Roundy: Suddenly it came to me. Oh, yes, I understand, it is this; when our Spirits entered our mortal bodies we lost the knowledge we had in the pre-existent state and you and your followers, not having the privilege of entering mortal bodies, retained that knowledge, therefore, you knew from the beginning the life-mission of all the great men.

Lucifer: Yes, he said, and we in every instance try to destroy them so as to prevent God's work through them.

Roundy: I have believed for many years it was you that sought to destroy Moses, Cyrus, Abraham, The Saviour and Joseph Smith while they were young, but you failed, did you not?

Lucifer: Yes, I did, but we know and understand Jesus's plan and doctrines just as well or better than do the Saints. We are just as perfectly organized as you, and are working more faithful than you are.

Roundy: Yes, so I understand, and I also understand that you send out missionaries, hold your conferences, receive reports, etc., that you also have a priesthood.

Lucifer: Yes, I have a priesthood. We send our agents out two and two as you do. We send our best informed to the authorities who preside over the people, also around the temples to discourage the temple work. We also hold our conferences, hear reports, attend to the business and pair them off and send them out again.

Roundy: I said, while you hold a priesthood you must obey the priesthood of God. Must you not? In answering this question he emphasized it very much and said:

Lucifer: ONLY WHEN IT IS EXERCISED IN FAITH, do I.

Roundy: Then as your agents travel among the people, you and your agents know everything that is going on, don't you?

especially among the Latter-day Saints—know all about their financial condition, social relations, etc.?

Lucifer: Yes, my agents have all things necessary and report to me.

Roundy: Then with this knowledge in your possession you are the author of spiritualism, mediumism, slate writings and all things connected therewith.

Lucifer: Yes sir, we have all knowledge necessary, and we can impersonate and imitate any person, so, when the spiritualists call for a certain person, my servants answer, having the information required.

Roundy: You said in the beginning of this conversation that it was your mission to destroy the works of Jesus Christ. Now with the perfect organization that you have, you are, as it has been said, everywhere present. Is this true?

Lucifer: Yes, it is our mission to overthrow all that leads to purity and Godliness, and we are everywhere present, especially in the sick room where the priesthood is, we are there to offset their power, and as thoughts are seeds sown, we do all we can to put evil thoughts into the minds of the people, especially the young; then teach them to cultivate those evil thoughts as they grow up to manhood and womanhood.

When the Sons of God met I was present, and when God would have you do good, we cause you to think evil. This has been our mission from the beginning, to OVERCOME good with evil. We knew when Joseph Smith was to come and we did all in our power to destroy him, but failed. Also you claim you must overcome evil with good. This is the conflict called the battle of the end, the time of times of the End.

Roundy: Do you believe that all the Latter-day Saints are seeking the glory of God?

Lucifer: No sir, I do not. All, who are seeking the praise of man, the pleasure of the world, and the almighty dollar, are coming my way and that is the majority of them. . . .

Roundy: 6000 years was the time allotted you for the establishment of your kingdom, was it not?

Lucifer: Yes sir, that was, or is, the allotted time.

Roundy: Then you must know that your end is near.

Lucifer: Yes, I do, but I want to tell you before I am bound, every person that can be led astray will be, and as far as I can, I am going to accomplish my work through the women from now on, and everything in this world will be turned upside down before I am bound [See *Revelation 20:1-3*. The "chain" by which Satan is bound means the Priesthood coming down from Heaven].

Roundy: . . . I will say he did not seem to become vexed at any time during our conversation. Just how long it lasted I cannot tell. It seems about one-half the night. I did not see him come or leave.

S. H. ROUNDY, (Signed)[54]

Satan will be bound by the chains of the Priesthood and through the righteousness of the people during Christ's millennial reign. Lucifer, who has "sought . . . the misery of mankind" (2 Nephi 2:18) and the "destruction of his agency" (see Moses 4:3) since the earliest beginnings in pre-mortality, desires "to deceive and to blind men, and to lead them captive . . . even as many as would not hearken unto [the Lord's] voice" (Moses 4:4) that he might destroy the work of the Lord and inhibit the exaltation of men.

Satan has great power to tempt and beguile and he uses all the means at his disposal to darken minds, deceive, distort, misrepresent and falsify truth as only the great imitator can. He counterfeits gospel truth with cleverly disguised false doctrines. "The father of all lies" (2 Nephi 2:18) is skilled at deception simply because of the eons of practice he has had.

The Saints can protect themselves by striving to obtain the spiritual gifts of discernment needed to recognize the counterfeits of Satan and void his entrapments. Because discernment is a gift of the Lord, granted through the Holy Ghost, it can only be expected by those who seek it and who are listening to the counsel of the Latter-day prophets and church leaders, searching the scriptures, and actively striving to obey the commandments of the Lord. Those who seek and obtain this gift will be less likely to be led astray by false doctrines and the enticements of false spirits.

President Harold B. Lee has said that the Saints will be able to detect truth from error by following the eternal principles of the gospel and searching for righteousness:

> Satan and his hosts were cast out because he set about to destroy the agency of man, and he became the author of falsehood to deceive and to blind men and to lead captive all who would not hearken to the words and teachings of God's eternal plan . . .
>
> . . . There has ever been, and ever will be, a conflict between the forces of truth and error; between the forces of righteousness and the forces of evil . . .
>
> So likewise, it is inspired wisdom that our efforts must be spent in teaching truth by the power of Almighty God, thus we can forge the most powerful of all weapons against the vicious doctrines of Satan.
>
> . . . The great danger in any society is apathy and a failure to be alert to the issues of the day . . .
>
> By the light of gospel truths we can be shown that "every thing which inviteth to do good, and to persuade to believe in Christ . . . ye may know with a perfect knowledge it is of God" (Moroni 7:16).
>
> But also we may know that "whatsoever thing persuadeth men to do evil, and believe not in Christ, and deny him, and serve not God, then ye may know with a perfect knowledge it is of the devil" (Moroni 7:17), whether it be labeled religion, philosophy, science, or political dogma.[55]

Chapter Five

WITCHCRAFT, A NEW AGE RELIGION

This chapter will show that many people who adhere to New Age principles belong to powerful and influential organizations which wield extensive political power. Many are part of a network of organizations which desires "the ushering in of a New Age of global peace and prosperity in which man becomes divine (gods) and occult principles govern the world."[56]

Gary Kah comments:

> This network is composed of the secret societies, hundreds of quasi-secret occult organizations (which the secret societies seem to influence), and a multitude of idealistic groups that have naively joined the cause in pursuit of world peace, or to help solve other "world problems.[57]

Kah was a high-ranking government liaison who received the Governor's Commendation for outstanding service to the State of Indiana, the A. C. Wall Street Journal Award for Outstanding Economic Achievement, and was listed in *Who's Who of Emerging Leaders in America*. He had a successful government career which took him around the world dealing with American embassies, foreign government officials, international business leaders, and, at times, members of the press and media. He became aware through his high-level contacts of plans that were being laid worldwide for the founding of a one-world government, most generally referred to by insiders as the "New World Order." Because of his background in government he was invited to join the World Constitution and Parliament Association to oversee the planning and implementation of the one world government. Kah stated that his investigation required more than ten thousand hours of research and ultimately extended around the world, from Taiwan to Israel to the Soviet Union.

> ... I also became aware of preparations being made for the New World Order here in the United States. I soon realized that this movement was not only economic in nature, but also contained a political dimension, and indeed, a spiritual motivation. I found the inter-connections between the three to be extensive.
> ... We are rapidly being pushed toward a one-world government by powerful Luciferic forces rooted in age-old secret societies.
> These forces, incredibly evil in intent, fully expect to accomplish their mission during the 1990s. I myself have had a rare glimpse into the forming of the world government by being involved in organizations participating in this effort. One of these organizations is the World Constitution and Parliament Association (WCPA) whose plans and documents [Kah has] reproduced.[58]

Peter Lalonde, author and publisher of a Christian newsletter on Bible prophecy called *The Omega Letter*, explains how New Age teachings will prepare the way for the anti-Christ:

> Today through the New age revival of "Mystery Babylon" people are becoming deceived into believing that they have godlike innate powers and abilities which they are just beginning to tap into. Such widespread acceptance of the paranormal could well pave the way for spiritual events that could trigger the birth of the New World Order and prepare the way for its charismatic leader.[59]

A New Ager who is practicing the occult and Eastern mysticism believes that he has a higher consciousness and powers which come from a close relationship to unseen spirits and forces. Such individuals can wield considerable psychic power, so that many can perform "miracles" through the power of Satan. Such fulfill the Biblical prophecy that in the last days ". . . false Christs and false prophets shall rise, and shall shew signs and wonders, to seduce, if it were possible, the elect" (Mark 13:22).

Miriam Starhawk, a prominent witch and past president of the Covenant of the Goddess, a union of New Age, pagan, and goddess traditions officially recognized as a church in California, affirms the similarities between witchcraft and Eastern beliefs:

> Witchcraft is a religion. . . . Only in this century have witches been able to "come out of the closet" . . . and counter the imagery of evil with truth. . . . To reclaim the word "witch" is to reclaim our right . . . to know the lifespirit within as divine.
>
> The longing for expanded consciousness has taken many of us on a spiritual "journey to the East" and to Hindu, Taoist, and Buddhist concepts. . . . Eastern religions offer a radically different approach to spirituality than Judeo-Christian traditions. . . . Their goal is not to know God, but to be God. In many ways these philosophies are very close to that of witchcraft.[60]

Witchcraft and Illuminati— Ties to the New Age Movement

Having shown the compatibility of New Age and witchcraft philosophies, let's briefly look at the connections that exist between witchcraft and certain powerful world leaders. A witchcraft insider by the name of John Todd has detailed his birth into a family of witches and subsequent rise to a position of extreme power and authority as a Grand Druid on the Council of Thirteen.

Todd said that as he grew up he thought that witchcraft was just another religion, like being a Baptist or a Catholic. He believed in a system of Gods and Goddesses and psychic powers, and that was all—which is where most witches stand.

During the process of studying witchcraft Todd began to learn what most witches don't know: that the Gods that lower witches worship do not exist. They are imitated by what the Saints call familiar spirits, spirit guides or demons. The higher witches recognize that they have only one god, and that god's name is Lucifer.[61]

According to Todd, the Council of Thirteen only takes orders from the Rothschilds (a group of private international bankers) for they are the Rothschild's private priesthood.[62] In his elevated position Todd became familiar with the organizational structure of a group of powerful and secretive men known as the Illuminati, whose religion is witchcraft.[63] He became privy to some of their inner workings, history, achievements and future designs for the world.

Keep in mind that the leaders in witchcraft are motivated by the same forces and players that drive the New Age Movement. Both movements are authored by Satan, and a "house divided against itself cannot stand" (Matthew 12:25). Expect New Age organizations to work in concert with organizations run through witchcraft. Both are extensions of the same devil, and differ simply in outward observances.

The Organization and Religion of the Illuminati

Texe Marrs explains that "what these men [the Illuminati] are doing is setting the stage for a great deception. They have organized the whole world into a theater of illusion. The whole world has become the lie. In effect, the religion of the Illuminati is witchcraft."[64]

The Illuminati's "goal was to hide the sciences of Witchcraft behind philanthropy, [and] destroy Christianity with humanism *(atheism)*, then set up a One World Government."[65] These are the same doctrines and philosophies of humanism that are being promoted by the New Age Movement.

In his exposé on the Illuminati, William Josiah Sutton explains some of their founding history:

> History books tell us that the French Revolution first began in 1787 or 1789, depending on which book you read. However, it was actually planned by Dr. Adam Weishaupt and the House of Rothschild almost 20 years before the Revolution took place.

Dr. Adam Weishaupt produced the blue print of it, while the House of Rothschild provided the money. This Apostle of Lucifer, Adam Weishaupt, was born a Jew, converted to Catholicism, then turned to Witchcraft, where he became an expert, and founded another sect of the Illuminati. This sect of Illuminati was founded May 1, 1776. Like Freemasonry, the Illuminati is a Luciferian movement to preserve and promote the ancient Black Arts of Babylonian and Druid Witchcraft. Its goals are to destroy Christianity and all world governments, and then unite them under a one world government whose ruler is Lucifer.[66]

The Illuminati's influence has so grown that for much of this century its symbol has appeared on American currency. According to Todd, the pyramid seal on the back of the one-dollar bill is the seal of the Illuminati. Americans are told that it is the reverse side of the great seal of the United States. However, the United States has never sealed a document with it and never intends to. The seal was in existence before the United States came to be, for it symbolizes the Illuminati. Above a pyramid is a glowing capstone that shows an eye inside. The capstone is the Rothschild family or tribunal that rules the Illuminati, for they were the creators of it. The eye is Lucifer, their God and their voice.[67] Stan Deyo, an investigator into this world-wide conspiracy, asks, "What does a pyramid have to do with the United States of America? Why does the pyramid have no capstone? Why is the 'eye of God's wisdom' shown inside a triangle? Why are there 13 steps in the pyramid?"[68]

At the top of the left seal on the back of the bill are the words "Annuit Coeptis" which are usually translated "Announcing the birth, creation or arrival." At the bottom of the pyramid is the number MDCCLXXVI representing the year 1776. This does not refer to the 4th of July but to May 1, 1776, the day Adam Weishaupt created the Illuminati.[69] At the bottom of the seal are the words "Novus Ordo Seclorum" which are translated as "New Secular Order!"[70] (New Secular Order can also be interpreted to mean New World

Order.)[71] Researcher Stan Deyo, who has exposed many of the Illuminati's plans, explains that mysticists translate the Latin in context as "Announcing the arrival of a new secret order of this age," and "The Established Order of the Ages Looks Favourably Upon our Endeavours."[72]

The American Illuminati

The American name for the Illuminati is The Council on Foreign Relations, according to Todd . Every member who sits on the CFR or the Trilateral Commission is an initiated member of the Illuminati.[73]

For 16 years Rear Admiral Chester Ward was a member of The Council on Foreign Relations which has included in its ranks U. S. Presidents, Vice-Presidents, Secretaries of State, Secretaries of Defense, CIA directors, in addition to business, media, and other giant economic leaders. He said that their goal was "to bring about the surrender of the national sovereignty and the national independence of the United States"[74]:

> The most powerful clique in these elitist groups have an objective in common—they want to bring about the surrender of the United States.
>
> A second clique of . . . members in the CFR . . . comprises the Wall Street International bankers and their key agents.
>
> Primarily, they want the world banking monopoly from whatever power ends up in control of global government.[75]

These powerful government and business leaders are working hard to eliminate national sovereignty, which severely limits their ability to seize more power. They do not care by what means world government comes, so long as they are in power when it does. While testifying before the Senate Foreign Relations Committee on February 17, 1950, CFR member James Warburg stated that "We shall have world government whether or not you like it—by conquest or consent."[76]

Longtime U. S. Senator Barry Goldwater had the following to say about the CFR and the like-minded Trilateralists and their objectives for the United States:

> We stand in danger of losing [our] freedom—not to a foreign tyrant, but to those well-meaning but misguided elitist utopians. . . .
>
> Whereas the Council on Foreign Relations is distinctly national in membership, the Trilateral Commission is international. Representation is allocated equally to Western Europe, Japan, and the United States. It is intended to be the vehicle for the multinational consolidation of the commercial and banking interest by seizing control of the political government of the United States. Zbigniew Brzezinski and David Rockefeller screened and selected every individual who was invited to participate in shaping and administering the proposed New World Order. . . . The Trilateral Commission represents a skillful, coordinated effort to seize control and consolidate the four centers of power—political, monetary, intellectual, and ecclesiastical. What the Trilateralists truly intend is the creation of a worldwide economic power superior to the political governments of the nation-states involved. . . . As managers and creators of the system they will control the future.[77]

A Managed Crisis:
Strikes, Riots, Revolution and U.S. Takeover Planned

These powerful global elitists are not satisfied with achieving their goals through a natural course of events. They are using a method called *"management by crisis"* to move their timetable foreword. Their objective is to identify or create crises, then propose "solutions" that would have never been accepted otherwise. A "managed crisis" has three stages. First, those who want a change in a particular direction, and who have adequate resources, present a crisis to the public. The crisis can be fabricated, or an existing crisis can be embraced. Next, the crisis is widely publicized. When there is enough public alarm, the "managers" propose their academically acclaimed solution to the crisis.

Management by crisis can concernably be executed through earthshattering events, but it is used mostly on a smaller scale, in a philosophy of *piecemeal functionalism*. This philosophy has been employed by many international groups, including the CFR and Trilateral Commission. In the April 1974 issue of *Foreign Affairs* the CFR journal, (p. 558), Richard Gardner stated that the New World Order "will have to be built from the bottom up rather than from the top down. It will look like a great 'booming, buzzing confusion,'...but an end run around national sovereignty, eroding it piece by piece, will accomplish much more than the old-fashioned frontal assault."[78]

Zbigniew Brzezinski, one of the organizers of the Trilateral Commission, explained how the piecemeal approach will be more effective in breaking down national sovereignty:

> In general, the prospects for achieving effective international cooperation can often be improved if the issues can be kept separate—what we now call piecemeal functionalism. . . . Coalitions of specialists can be built across national boundaries in specific functional areas, blunting the nationalism that otherwise might hinder agreement. . . .[79]

Peter Lalonde explains the origins of this philosophy:

> The concept of piecemeal functionalism was originally codified by the Aspen Institute's Harland Cleveland. He observed that trying to directly create a New World Order through large all-encompassing organizations such as the U.N. has not worked. By employing the concept of piecemeal functionalism these groups expect to achieve much broader success. By appearing to address separate issues piece by piece, treaty by treaty, law by law, issue by issue, and organization by organization, the New World Order is in fact being assembled virtually unnoticed.[80]

New Age leader Mark Satin celebrates the effectiveness of this piecemeal gradualism:

> The new politics is arising out of the . . . social movements of our time: the feminist, environmental, spiritual, human potential . . . and world order movements. . . . The contributions come together like the pieces of an intricate jigsaw puzzle.[81]

A good example of piecemeal gradualism in the United States is the implementation of Executive Orders over the years. An Executive Order is not a law passed by Congress, nor a ruling by the Supreme Court or any other court. It is a decree issued by the President and entered in the Federal Register. It becomes law 15 days after its entry—law just as valid as one passed by the congress or approved by the Supreme Court. Various Executive Orders on the books essentially give the President the right to control crises (or a "managed crisis" that was created) by suspending the Constitution and Congress, declaring marshal law and calling out the military if he views the need under a "national emergency."

Liberty Lobby, an organization dedicated to American freedom defines Executive Orders:

> The Federal Register is probably the most powerful document printed in the United States today. What appears in its columns as notification of official Presidential actions assumes the power of law. No congressional authorization is required. . . . There is no review by the judiciary. Executive orders are laws made by one man—The President. The fact is, Executive Orders are never approved by Congress! They have the "force of the law" WITHOUT legislation! The president could declare a 'national emergency' on his own and then invoke these orders! . . .
>
> Through certain Executive Orders it would be possible for one man to completely ignore the Constitution, the authority of Congress, and the will of the people. Through implementation of these Executive Orders a complete dictatorship can be imposed.
>
> There are already such Executive Orders.[82]

Eleven Executive Orders have been combined into one, EO 11490, which provides for complete Presidential takeover of all communications, all fuels, power and minerals, all food resources and farms, all modes of transportation control of highways, seaports, railroads, inland waterways, aircraft and airports, and public storage facilities. They also provide for the mobilization of all civilians into work brigades under government supervision and government takeover of all health, education and welfare functions. It designates the Postmaster General to operate a national registration of all persons. It also provides for the authority to relocate communities, build new housing with public funds, designate areas to be abandoned as unsafe and establish new locations for populations.[83]

The full implications of this vast power can be known when it is realized that for many years, a group of 100 individuals led by Rexford G. Tugwell have had plans that call for the elimination of the Constitution of the United States of America and its replacement with a "New Constitution."[84] It calls for the establishment of an elite decision-making cadre made up of insiders.

The *National Spotlight*, a conservative newspaper, sums up the New Constitution thus:

> Tugwell and his cohorts declared the U. S. Constitution is an ambiguous document concocted 200 years ago and inadequate for the present day. The New Constitution would abolish states and substitute a smaller number of regions, called republics. They wouldn't be republics in any rational sense of the word. [They] . . . would be mere administrative eunuchs, having little real power beyond the paperwork assigned them from above. The "Illuminated" ones on top would be calling the tune.[85]

President John Taylor, speaking of the dangers to the Constitution by wicked and corrupt men, commented on the Prophet Joseph Smith's prophecy:

> "The Constitution of the United States was given by inspiration of God." But good, virtuous and holy principles may be

perverted by corrupt and wicked men. The Lord was opposed by Satan, Jesus had his Judas, and this nation abounds with traitors who ignore that sacred palladium of liberty and seek to trample it under foot.[86]

Erastus Snow was another church leader who repeated the Prophet Joseph's belief that the Constitution would be put in great danger by conspiring men:

> . . . We were told by the prophet Joseph Smith, that the United States Government and people would undermine one principle of the Constitution after another, until its whole fabric would be torn away, and that it would become the duty of the Latter-day Saints and those in sympathy with them to rescue it from destruction, and to maintain and sustain the principles of human freedom for which our fathers fought and bled. We look for these things to come in quick succession.[87]

As can be seen, our prophets and leaders have foreseen the powerful influences that would seek to dismantle our Constitution and destroy our freedoms. The Lord said he established the constitution ". . . by the hands of wise men whom [He] raised up" (D & C 101:80) and ". . . suffered to be established, and should be maintained for the rights and protection of all flesh, according to just and holy principles;" (D & C 101:77). Without the present Constitution our inherent and God-given rights of free agency can be severely restricted.

In order to understand the seriousness of this threat, consider the words of another prophet, David O. McKay, and his counsel to the Saints concerning free agency and their obligation to preserve this God-given gift:

> Next to the bestowal of life itself, the right to direct that life is God's greatest gift to man. Among the immediate obligations and duties resting upon members of the Church, and one of the most urgent and pressing for attention and action of all liberty-loving people is the preservation of individual liberty. Freedom of choice is more to be treasured than any possession earth can

give. It is inherent in the spirit of man. It is a divine gift to every normal being. Whether born in abject poverty or shackled at birth by inherited riches, everyone has this most precious of all life's endowments—the gift of free agency, man's inherited and inalienable right.[88]

Are Christians Such a Threat to the New Age?

There is another law called the Genocide Treaty (known as Public Law 100-606—November 4, 1988, Chapter 50A—Genocide).[89] Under this law, an individual can be put in federal prison for converting somebody from the faith that they were born into. In other words, if someone converts a Catholic, a Jew, or a witch, and their parents press charges, he can be sent to federal prison for doing so.

The proposal had been defeated in Congress for many years but was signed into law in 1988 by Ronald Reagan. It is a binding U.S. treaty and as such it not only makes nations and their leaders answerable to the World Court, but every citizen as well. Its wording makes it feasible to interpret an act of genocide as being one person inducing "mental harm" to someone of a different religious belief inasmuch as that person is "a member" of another group.

Concerning the supreme authority of treaty law, Article VI, paragraph 2 of the United States Constitution states:

> *This Constitution, and the Laws of the United States which shall be made in Pursuance thereof; and all treaties made, or which shall be made, under the Authority of the United States, shall be the supreme Law of the Land; and the judges in every State shall be bound thereby, any thing in the constitution or Laws of any state to the Constitution notwithstanding.*

The U.S. Supreme Court has also upheld the view that treaty law *supersedes* domestic law, the Constitution and the Bill of Rights.[90] Thus, if a Latter-day Saint youth is sent to another country on a mission, and he bears his testimony to another person and somehow hurts that person's feelings, he could conceivably then be tried by the World Court without the protection of the U.S. Bill of Rights. This is not confined exclusively to a foreign mission either—it could conceivably happen in any town in the U.S. as well.[91]

With this law on the books and the contentious, litigious state of today's society, it does not take much imagination to see what kind of suits could be filed against missionary-minded religions in the near future. Considering the increasing state of hostility toward religion, mere proselytizing may come to be perceived as "causing mental anguish" and as such will be seen as an intolerable, divisive action in the New Age New World Order that is developing.

Concerning the deterioration of religious liberties, John Daniel points out that eight of ten steps needed to destroy Christian America have already been successful and the ninth will be the "anti-proselyting" law. The French have already set the precedent with a law forbidding those in their public schools from even extending the invitation to attend church. If this type of law were to become fully enacted in America and Christians resisted it, then the tenth step could come into play quickly: the planned elimination of those who resist the satanic New Age blueprint for America. A "Reign of Terror," similar to those successfully used during the French and Russian Revolutions, could again be used successfully if morality continues to decline, and if a large-enough crisis makes this option popular among the majority. Satan has accomplished this many times throughout history, even in the "sophisticated" Twentieth Century. In light of the persecutions prophesied by John, it can be assumed that Satan hopes to do the same thing to Christians that he has done to other minorities in the past.[92]

In a society that already labels good as bad and bad as good, Satan has laid much of the groundwork needed to create great persecutions of the LDS church and Christianity in general. Christians are already attacked for their "outdated" religious beliefs by atheists, homosexuals, radical feminists, abortionists, environmentalists, secular humanists, socialists, globalists, Marxists, New Agers and others. Christians are criticized by the media and others sympathetic to the New Age movement for demanding high moral values such as patriotism, loyalty, bravery, chastity, protection for the unborn and decency in movies and television. If Christian-bashing continues to grow, America's thinking may be polarized until all believers in Jesus Christ will literally be on the outside looking in. Because of a newly created majority hostile to Christian values, tolerance of divergent views could disappear for those whose views encompass a belief in Jesus Christ.

Investigation of New Age literature shows that many New Agers sanction and even promote the persecution of Christians as a necessary part of the coming new age of enlightenment. They justify their position by explaining that this must happen before a spiritual uniting of humanity can come about. Accordingly, those who are not converted to this New Age of enlightenment and refuse to accept its definition of world unity, love and harmony will need to be silenced or removed in order to usher in their version of peace on earth. In 1981, at one of their meetings, a spokesman for Transcendental Meditation (TM) admitted that the entire mission of TM was to counter the ever-spreading demon of Christianity.[93]

New Age writer Barbara Marx Hubbard expressed the New Age view of other religions quite succinctly:

> People who do not accept the New Age teaching [including Bible-believing Christians] are an evolutionary drag on humanity and must capitulate or be killed.[94]

Hubbard is hardly alone in her harsh, unbending views. Texe Marrs has recorded statements of several prominent New Agers that outline the death sentence for those deemed unfit to enter into the New Age era of peace and joy:[95]

> Dr. Christopher Hyatt predicts that the New Age will come to pass only after bloodletting and pain on a mass scale.[96] Djwhal Khul, Alice Bailey's "Tibetan Master," says that one-third of all humanity must die by the year 2000.[97] John Randolph Price was told by his spirit guide that up to two and one-half billion might perish in the coming chaos![98] Ruth

Montgomery's books predict that turmoil and destruction will be visited on millions who will pass on into spirit.[99] Meanwhile, Maharishi Mahesh Yogi warns that "the unfit and ignorant won't survive."[100]

Remember, the New Age embraces the same type of superstitious Babylonian mystery teachings that prevailed during the Dark Ages. Today analytical inquiry could slowly decrease as supernatural darkness increases. These altered states of consciousness can lead to violent acts when subjects submit to the will of the satanic spirit that they have invited in. Marrs explains how dangerous altered states of consciousness can be if a demon takes control:

> The New Age practice of occult meditation leaves the individual in a semiconscious trance state and easily susceptible to influence by demonic spirits. Christopher Hyatt describes the process of Eastern Meditation as "emptying oneself out: a spiritual laxative."[101] Once you've emptied your mind, it can be quickly filled up by unholy spirits. That's what demon possession is all about.
>
> Once the person is indwelt by demons, he or she becomes like putty in their master's cruel hands. When he gives the order for them to take to the streets, they will obey. When the demon spirit whips up an attitude of violence and unrepressed hostility, it must be ventilated.
>
> Satan's New Age followers will one day soon ventilate that hostility against the People of Light, God's people. . . . Jose Arguelles, head of the New Age's Harmonic Convergence, has spoken of a coming "purification period" in which the "people's army of earth" will "de-structure civilization" and dismantle the present world economy. This army is to be made up of "superhumans" whose minds are linked up with "spirit guides" from another dimension.[102] In truth, these will be New Age warriors taking direct orders from demons. Warriors who curse the light. They will be Soldiers of Darkness.[103]

New Age followers within the U.S. Army have formed an elite New Age military unit called the "First Earth Battalion." It was founded by Lieutenant Colonel Jim Channon, and is steeped in New Age Occult teachings and the martial arts. The following is taken from a letter by a soldier in that New Age Battalion, written to Texe Marrs and published in his newsletter *Flashpoint*, September 1994:

> We were a group of highly selective soldiers. We were to be "Purified Psychic soldiers." We all had our outline of "The Plan." We were to prepare for the emergence of a "New Order." We were encouraged to read all types of New Age and Occult books, to study various martial arts, and to practice mind powers. Spirit Guide (demon) communication was also encouraged. They were said to be "wiser." My best friend and I studied and practiced our meditation and psychic warrior skills everyday. I also studied Ninjutsu and Tai Kwon Do, as well as Tai Chi. We weren't supposed to talk to a lot of people about this unit as of then.
>
> I am holding the instruction books now and will quote to you directly from them. At the end of the 11th Delta Force Conference, the instructor said, ". . . I knew with sudden certainty that I had been a witness to a process of unique valor and majesty; an army of Excellence." After the casting of the eight Runes he said, "I offer you this element of ceremony with my own promise of devotion and my gratitude: The blessing upon all who have arrived at the place of termination and new beginnings."
>
> We were told of this "Third Wave World" and that we must prepare locally until the call goes out for global action. We were told that we were the soldiers who had the power to make paradise. That we were a "leaderless but powerful network." It doesn't take much imagination to guess who the "new leader" is to be.
>
> As for our potential to grow, we were told we could "become as gods," that there are no limits for a First Earth Battalion soldier. We could travel to new places in our minds,

walk through fire, move and/or bend objects with our minds, stop our hearts with no ill effects, and see into the future, etc., etc., etc.

More quotes; "We shall continue to look everywhere to find methods of control." "In the end, all martial arts serve only one real function, to open the warrior-soldier up to the truth: that is when the spirit can come in."

There are six levels of Psychic Soldier, from the new trainee to the highest, which is the *Warrior Monk* or *Master Warrior*. Then it's on to spiritual beings (like angels) and on to gods. Our combat was called the "Beginning of the Beginning." We were confidently told: "any Nation or Army that ignores the New Ingredients will suffer strange defeats. They may win some battles but we will win the war. Our organized military forces are the perfect catalysts for this action. Evolution is God's promise that men shall be gods. We are all one as God."

The New Age military force requires rituals, chants, OM meditation, Earth prayers, and a pledge of allegiance to the planet and to people (no mention of the U.S.). The first book of required reading was *The Aquarian Conspiracy*. Then on to many others.

. . . In the service, as you know, the lower ranking people are usually young and programmed to listen to and obey anyone who outranks them. Well, if you could see my New Age military instruction manuals and books, you would see all the names of leaders listed are either high ranking civilians or high ranking officers. There is a lot of push behind all that brass.

I am still in the military, and it worries me that our military can be so readily swayed by New Age thinking.[104] (Emphasis added.)

Many of these high-ranking leaders are hostile toward traditional religion and have obtained power in highly influential government organizations. One such agency is discussed in the 8/94 edition of the McAlvany Intelligence Advisor. Donald S. McAlvany reveals the nature of several anti-Christian regulations that have been proposed during the Clinton Administration:

The new anti-Christian, anti-religious regulations proposed by the Equal Employment Opportunity Commission (EEOC) [are] the most incredible examples yet of the coming socialist/regulatory dictatorship and the anti-Christian agenda of the socialists and the New World Order. And even though both Houses of Congress have overwhelmingly voted on resolutions to condemn the guidelines, the EEOC can still push them through by regulatory fiat.

The EEOC is the government body that interprets federal civil rights law and sets the standards for what is permissible or unacceptable in the workplace. McAlvany states that according to the office of Senator Hank Brown (R-CA), the following actions would have been prohibited under EEOC guidelines had they been allowed to stand:

1. Wearing a cross around the neck, wrist or any openly visible part of the body.
2. Wearing a yarmulke (yarmulkeh); Orthodox Jews wear the head covering seven days a week.
3. Displaying a picture of Christ on an office desk or wall.
4. Wearing a T-shirt, hat or other clothing that has any religious emblem or phrasing on its face.
5. Displaying a Bible or other religious book on a desk, or making it openly visible in a work or lounge area.
6. Hosting Christmas, Hanukkah, Thanksgiving or Easter celebrations, parties, or events that have any focus on Christ, God or other religious connotations in any form.
7. Celebrations or parties which have any religious focus or reference.
8. Opening or closing prayers or invocations at a company program, banquet, celebration or event.
9. Sharing your faith and speaking to other employees about religion.
10. Nativity displays or scenes.
11. Inviting a fellow employee to a synagogue, church, temple or other place of worship.

12. Conversations about religion or religious groups, functions and events.
13. Prayer breakfasts.
14. Singing or humming a religious song while at a copy machine.
15. Serving only pork or beef at a company Fourth of July picnic.
16. Having a local church choir or school choir come in for a Christmas celebration and sing any song which makes reference to Christ, God or any religion or religious principle.
17. Telling any joke (regardless of the innocence of the subject matter or intent) that refers to any religion or religious group whatsoever.
18. Giving a fellow employee a holiday card, birthday card, get well card, greeting card or plaque which includes any religious reference.
19. Making reference to Christ, God or any religious figure or subject matter in a company mission, plan or goal statement.
20. Praying while in the work place.
21. The display of calendars or "thoughts of the day" books which make reference to Scripture or religious sayings.
22. Displaying any religious artwork, book, devotional, figure, symbol or trinket in an openly visible area.
23. Hosting a Bible study or other religious gathering.
24. Company uniform and work apparel requirements.
25. Almost any form of religious expression in the work place.[105]

This mentality of the New Age proponents is especially alarming to Latter-day Saints in light of statements like these of New Age adherent Mortimer J. Adler:

> World peace is impossible without world government. World government is impossible to establish and prosper without world community. And world community requires a certain degree of cultural unity, a condition that certainly does not exist at present.

> We have no problem at all if religion does not claim to involve knowledge and it is not concerned with what is true and what is false. If, however, it claims to involve knowledge . . . [and it claims that] *it alone has its source in divine revelation, accepted by an act of faith that is in itself divinely caused* . . . [and if] religion claims to be supernatural knowledge—knowledge *that man has only as a gift from God* . . . then we are confronted with a special problem. . . .[106] (Emphasis added.)

The Church of Jesus Christ of Latter-day Saints and other Christians are already viewed as a major impediment to the New Age and One World government proponents, as well we should be. If religions that are "accepted by an act of faith" are a "special problem," this would necessitate the elimination of the problem, as many New Ager's have already proposed. It is clear that the New Age concept of "world peace" cannot be achieved until all Christians are eliminated, along with the rest of the un-cooperative segments of the world who refuse to accept the envisioned "cultural unity." Could this be why Satan and his church will be making "war with the saints" (See Revelation 13:4)?

Could those who are followers of Satan become so powerful that they will shed the blood of whomever fights the anti-Christ and his satanic One World organization?

Pastor Robert Rosio, founder of Cheswich Christian Academy, sums up the growing anti-Christian sentiment:

> We now are beginning to see the criminalization of Christianity. The Christian viewpoint not only will be unwelcome; eventually it will be illegal. New labels have appeared to redefine and thus justify sin. Homosexuality has become an "alternative lifestyle," or a "sexual preference." Abortion is no longer murder; it is now "the right to privacy." People are not called immoral or promiscuous. They are "sexually active." Pornography has been relabeled as "sexually explicit." At the same time, Christians are being labeled as extreme fundamentalists, narrow-minded, and judgmental bigots. In truth, however, the new morality is simply the old immorality relabeled, and

the reprobate mind is still a terminal condition. The things that promote lawlessness still will be judged, for God does not change. He is neither asleep nor unaware. He will not be mocked. As Billy Graham said, *"If God doesn't judge the United States, He will owe an apology to Sodom and Gomorrah."*[107] (Emphasis added.)

Not only could the realization of New Age goals result in physical dangers to Christians and others, but current deceptive practices of the New Age can already place Christians in grave danger spiritually.

Chapter Six

SATAN'S SYMBOLS AND MUSIC

Constance Cumbey, one of the earliest New Age whistleblowers, reveals this historical change in approach:

> ... these demonic messengers told [New Age occultists] to keep the society and teachings secret—at least for the time being. This was a dictum that was to prevail for 100 years—until 1975—the year initiates were at last permitted to make the initiatory teachings public.
>
> After the secrecy order came down, the Society began to communicate by secret signs and words of recognition. This practice continues today within the modern New Age Movement. It is specifically designed to keep information from hostile investigators.[108]

Much satanic jewelry was "revealed" by demons to those high in the occult. Until a few years ago it was impossible to buy most of this jewelry outside of a witchcraft store. They were handmade by silversmiths belonging to the occult priesthood and sold only to initiated witches in occult stores. Since then this symbolic jewelry has become commonplace in the New Age. Now, the Illuminati have decided that one of the greatest tricks they can play on Christians is to put this jewelry around their necks and on their hands. There could be many reasons for this, but one of the most compelling theories is that this jewelry attracts demons. Because

The Pentagram and Hexagram

When a witch wants to practice witchcraft she will sit or stand in a Pentagram, a five-pointed star in a circle. That is her strongest form of protection. She will then lay a six-pointed hexagram (named for its use in hexes, practicing black magic or casting a spell) on a circle on the floor. This causes demons to appear at her instruction.[109]

The Pentagram, a five-sided star in a circle, is the most evil and dangerous sign in witchcraft. With one point up it symbolizes witchcraft; two points up symbolizes demon worship or Satanism.[110] It is interesting to note that the Eastern Star symbol, associated with Freemasonry, is a two points up, five-pointed star. As mentioned earlier, *this symbolizes the goat head which Satanists believe is the representative of the devil.*[111]

The Goat Head Pentagram

William Josiah Sutton discussed one of the most common and evil symbols that is enjoying popularity:

> Instead of the satanic evil looking people of the Middle Ages, the witches of today have been, for the past century, portrayed as good people, who fight against the evil forces of this world, such as "Wonder Woman," with her sign of white magic (the Pentagram) displayed on her forehead. But to distinguish the bad witches from the good witches, say the occultists, a reversed Pentagram with *two points upward* is a symbol of Black Magic, and of those who do worship the Devil. The two points of the star pointed upwards suggests the horns of the Devil symbolized as a goat attacking the heavens with his horns. This five pointed star which has two points upwards was, and is today, worn as an amulet by open Devil worshippers, and by many modern day magicians and wizards. Originally this

evil sign was worn to show Satan that they had chosen him as their leader.

Is this not chilling and frightening to know that multitudes of women of high fashion may not be aware that when they wear that little gold chain around their neck, with this five pointed star with two points upward, they are showing they have chosen the devil's side, and seek his protection?[112]

The Star of David has only recently been called the Star of David. For thousands of years it was called the hexagram or the Crest of Solomon. The scriptures affirm that "Solomon did evil in the sight of the Lord" (1 Kings 11:6) and that "the Lord was angry with Solomon, because his heart was turned from the Lord God of Israel, which had appeared unto him twice" (1 Kings 11:9). Many of the New Age/Occult community credit King Solomon with refining many occult practices which are still in use today.

John Todd said many Christians are astonished when they are told that the greatest wizard (male witch) who ever lived was Solomon. When he backslid, he really backslid; as great as his writings were in the Christian Bible, his writings in the Witchcraft Bible are even more significant to the occult. The very initiation rights—how to prepare a Witchcraft Bible, how to conjure demons up, even how to commit human sacrifice—are writings that he created.[113]

Bible scholar Roy Allan Anderson spoke of Solomon's wickedness in his later years:

> When Solomon began to worship a form of this system of Satan's, it was primarily because of the pagan wives he married. "And he had seven hundred wives, princesses, and three hundred concubines: And his wives turned his heart. For it came to pass, when Solomon was old, that his wives turned away his heart after other gods: and his heart was not perfect with the Lord his God, as was the heart of David his father. For Solomon went after Ashtoreth the goddess of the Zidonians, and after Milcom the abomination of the children of Ammonites. And Solomon did evil in the sight of the Lord, and went not fully

after the Lord, as did David his father. Then did Solomon build a high place for Chemosh, the abomination of Moab, in the hill that is before Jerusalem, and for Molech, the abomination of the children of Ammon" (1 Kings 11:3-7).

Solomon, noted for his wisdom and understanding, who had been called "Jedidiah," which means "Beloved of the Lord" (2 Samuel 12:25), who wrote in his youth, "There is a way which seemeth right unto a man, but the end thereof are the ways of death," (Proverbs 14:12), because of his lust for Women and Wealth, eventually separated himself from the Lord and practiced the most abominable rites of paganism. It was Solomon who was the first of several kings of Israel to allow the sacrifice of little children.

This hill he built was in the valley of the son of Hinnom. This area lies at the entry of the east gate of Jerusalem (Jeremiah 19:2). In verses 5 and 6 of the same chapter we read:

"They have built also the high places of Baal, to burn their sons with fire for burnt offerings unto Baal, which I commanded not, nor spake it, neither came it into my mind: Therefore, behold, the days come, saith the Lord, that this place shall no more be called Tophet, nor The valley of the son of Hinnom, but The valley of slaughter."[114]

Elder Bruce R. McConkie confirms that Solomon in his apostate years, built repulsive paganistic idols where children were sacrificed to the despicable Gods of the heathen:

The valley of Hinnom was the scene of some of the most horrifying and abominable practices ever to defile Israel. It was here that Solomon built places for the worship of Molech; it was here that infant sacrifices were sponsored by those wicked kings, Ahaz and Manasseh; it was here that Josiah spread human bones and other corruptions; it was here (in Jesus' day) that garbage, dead animals, and human corpses were burned. This valley was both the cesspool of Jerusalem and the place where continuing fires burned the refuse of the city, giving rise to the use of the term *Ge Hinnom* or *Gehenna*, or land of Hinnom, as the symbol for the eternal fires of hell.[115]

Solomon apostatized from the Church, turned from the blessings of God, and embraced the abhorrent worship of idolatry. He embraced and worshiped false gods (1 Kings 11), immorality and the lusts of the flesh, and allowed the sacrifice of children to these false gods (1 Kings 11:7-8). The wisdom the Lord had given Solomon (1 Kings 5:12, 2 Chronicles 1:12) because of his righteousness (2 Chronicles 1:11) vanished as he turned from the covenants and statutes of the Lord.

The Ankh

The ankh, which looks like a cross with a loop on top, symbolizes a contempt for virginity and belief in fertility rites and worship of the Sun God Ra. *The Sun God Ra is the Egyptian name for Lucifer.*[116] The author has noted with interest that one of the major music companies has advertisements in its promotional literature for crystals, dragons, wizards on tee-shirts, incense to transport oneself to a blissful state, and the *cross/ankh* necklace which is described as a beautiful combination of two ancient symbols.

The Yin/Yang

Another popular New Age symbol—one that the author has seen several young Mormon girls wearing—is the *Yin/Yang*, an ancient Chinese symbol which stands for the unity of opposites: for example the unity of masculine and feminine and good and evil, etc. Only Satan would want to erase these distinctions. Rest assured those symbols carry no reverence for the Lord and Savior Jesus Christ.

The "Peace" Symbol

William Josiah Sutton explains the true meaning behind the "Peace Symbol" and its relationship to witchcraft:

> In many covens, before a witch can be initiated into the arts of Witchcraft, the initiate, if not born into a family of witches, must take a ceramic cross and turn it upside down, then break

the cross-bar downwards. This is to show other witches that they have rejected Christianity and Jesus Christ. Today, many ignorant people, who call themselves Christians, hold this sign up to show that they are for peace, when in reality it shows they have rejected Jesus. The reason the name *PEACE* was tagged on this evil sign is derived from the peace witches say they get after a new initiate shows his rejection of Christianity, and when he practices the arts of Witchcraft.[117]

What has been called the Peace Symbol for the last few decades has been called a broken cross for several centuries. This is reason enough to avoid this symbol, for it does not represent the type of peace desired by Christians.

The Unicorn's Horn

Another symbol used by the movement is called the Unicorn's Horn. Some vendors are currently calling it the Italian Horn so that people will buy it, for to the occult it signifies that you trust the devil for your finance.[118] If you don't trust the devil for your finance, don't wear it; it would supposedly have just the opposite effect for a Christian. If you have any unicorns or other satanic symbols around your home, play it safe, get rid of them.

Satanic Forms of Music

Satan's primary goal is to lead the hearts of men away from their Savior and onto forbidden paths. One of his most effective tools in recent decades has been forms of music that affect the listener's sensitivity and behavior. Satan has long noted the powerful effects of music, particularly its ability to alter mood and emotion. Noting music's power to inspire reverence, patriotism, sadness, romance, peace and war, Satan has inspired willing artists to create forms of music that inspire anger, rebellion, lust, selfishness, apathy, recklessness, violence, and submission.

Music Affects Behavior

Numerous studies indicate that certain types of music can have a dangerous influence on behavior. While many types of music can have negative influences, the main focus of this discussion will be on dangerous forms of rock and New Age music.

While not all forms of rock and New Age music are necessarily harmful, a substantial portion are Satanically inspired and hazardous to one's spiritual health. They are anthems of the religion of self-worship, hymns of self-indulgence and rebellion. Many were even specifically composed to prepare the listener for New Age/Satanic worship.

Scientists have noted the effects of music on plants, animals and humans. While the results of these studies have been widely interpreted, the data indicates a consistent pattern: certain types of music seem to enhance physical and mental health, while other types of music inhibit it. Scientists are still trying to understand why this is so, but enough is known that an entire field of study has grown out of such research. Many universities offer degrees in music therapy, and major hospitals have noted the effectiveness of music therapy when used in concert with other forms of treatment. Indeed, music does have measurable effects on the body, and the forms that produce the most negative effects are forms that children likely listen to. Below is a small sampling of scientific findings:

An article appearing in Salt Lake City's *Deseret News* reported a study showing the effects of music on lizards. This study by Teri Stokes showed that when exposed to classical music, lizards lifted their faces towards the source of the music and gained a gram of weight during the experiment. A different group, when exposed to Country Western music, lost a half-a-gram of weight, did not look up, paced back and forth and became agitated. They even hid their heads by burying themselves in the sand.[119]

In another study done with plants, Dorothy Retallack found that when exposed to rock music, petunias refused to bloom; however, classical music encouraged six new flowers in a group that bloomed beautifully. The plants exposed to rock music leaned away from the speakers, while those exposed to classical music leaned towards the sound. Zinnias showed similar behavior, with the noted addition that they also grew taller when exposed to classical music. At the end of a month all of the plants that were exposed to rock music died, while those exposed to classical or no music survived.[120]

Studies by John K. Diamond found that people can be invigorated, energized, and balanced by certain sounds and that overall health and well-being are affected by music. He found that people who repeatedly listened to rock music more frequently complained of weak muscles. Diamond hypothesized that a rock beat weakens the symmetry between the two halves of the brain, causing subtle perceptual difficulties and other early symptoms of stress. He also found that when children stopped listening to rock music while studying, their academic achievement improved considerably.[121]

Psychologist James Girard remarked:

> There is a rhythm in respiration, heart beat, speech, gait, etc. The cerebral hemispheres are in a perpetual state of rhythmic swing day and night. There must be a condition of harmony or perfect balance between the mental, emotional, and physical operations of the organism if it is to function properly. It is precisely at this point that rock music becomes potentially dangerous. This is because to maintain a sense of well-being and integration, it is essential that man is not subjected to too much of any body rhythms not in accord with his natural body rhythm.[122]

Frank Zappa, who was known as an oracle for the rock culture and as an advocate of the big beat, recognized the powerful, mood-altering aspects of rock music, noting its ability to work evil:

> The loud sounds and bright lights of today are tremendous indoctrination tools. Is it possible to modify the human's chemical structure with the right combination of frequencies? (Frequencies you can't hear are manifested as frequencies you can see in a light.) Can prolonged exposure to mixed media pro-

duce mutations? If the right kind of beat makes you tap your foot, what kind of beat makes you curl your fist and strike?

Suppose:

... you were out there dancing and sweating and really feeling the music (every muscle and fiber of your being, etc., etc.) and the music suddenly got louder and more vicious ... louder and viciouser than you could ever imagine (and you danced harder and got sweaty and feverish) and got your unsuspecting self worked up into a total frenzy, bordering on electric Buddha nirvana total acid freak cosmic integration (one with the universe), and you were drunk and hot and not really in control of your body or your senses (*you are possessed by the music*), and all of a sudden the music gets EVEN LOUDER ... and not only that: IT GETS FASTER AND YOU CAN'T BREATHE (But you can't stop either; it's impossible to stop) and you know you can't black out because it feels too good ... I ask you now, if you were drunk and all this stuff is happening all over the place and somebody (with all the best intentions in the world) MADE YOU STOP so he could ask you this question: "Is a force this powerful to be overlooked by a society that needs all the friends it can get?" Would you listen?[123]

Rev. James J. LeBar, Consultant on Cults for the Archdiocese of New York, agrees that one of the most potentially mood-altering elements in rock music is the beat, citing another author's observations:

> An indication of the validity of this premise comes from Bob Larson in his book, *Rock And Roll: The Devil's Diversion*. He tells of a missionary who took back to Africa with him records of semi-classical music and acid rock. He played both to members of the local tribe. When the semi-classical was played, the people responded with smiles and nods of approval, and they were generally calm and peaceful. Without comment the missionary switched to rock. Immediately their expressions changed, they became confused and agitated. Some grabbed their spears and were ready for war.

A variation of this is told by another missionary who brought back the rock music and was playing it in his own tent. The tribal chief came up to him and inquired why he was playing music to invoke the evil spirits. It seems that the beat of the music was exactly what the tribes used for the evil spirit dance.[124]

Our church leaders are concerned about the "evil effects of some popular music." Ezra Taft Benson, then of the Council of the Twelve, quoted a letter from a concerned father, Richard Nibley, whom Elder Benson described as "a well-informed teacher of youth," concerning corruptive influences in the rock scene:

> ... Satan knows that music hath charms to soothe or stir the savage beast. That music has power to create atmosphere has been known before the beginning of Hollywood. Atmosphere creates environment, and environment influences behavior—the behavior of Babylon or of Enoch.
>
> Music creates atmosphere. Atmosphere creates environment. Environment influences behavior. What are the mechanics of this process?
>
> *RHYTHM* is the most physical element in music. It is the only element in music that can exist in bodily movement without benefit of sound. A mind dulled by drugs or alcohol can respond to the beat.
>
> *LOUDNESS* adds to muddling the mind. Sound magnified to the threshold of pain is of such physical violence as to block the *higher processes of thought and reason.* (And turning down the volume of this destructive music does not remove the other evils.)
>
> *REPETITION* to the extreme is another primitive rock device....
>
> *GYRATIONS*, a twin to rock rhythm, are such that even clean hands and a pure heart cannot misinterpret their insinuations....
>
> *DARKNESS* (and dimmed lights) are another facet of the rock scene. It is a black mass that deadens the conscience in a

mask of anonymity. Identity lost in darkness shrinks from the normal feelings of responsibility.

STROBE LIGHTS split the darkness in blinding shafts that reduce resistance like the lights of an interrogator's third degree or the swinging pendulum of the hypnotist would control your behavior. . . .

The whole psychedelic design is a swinging door to drugs, sex, rebellion, and Godlessness. Combined with the screaming obscenities of the lyrics, this mesmerizing music has borne the fruit of filth. Leaders of the rock society readily proclaim their degeneracy. . . .

"For behold, at that day shall he [the devil] rage in the hearts of the children of men, and stir them up to anger against that which is good" (2 Nephi 28:20).

The speech of the rock festival is often obscene. Its music, crushing the sensibilities in a din of primitive idolatry, is in glorification of the physical to the debasement of the spirit. . . . The legendary orgies of Greece and Rome cannot compare to the monumental obscenities found in these cesspools of drugs, immorality, rebellion and pornographic sound. The famed Woodstock festival was a gigantic manifestation of a sick nation. Yet the lurid movie and rock recordings of its unprecedented filth were big business in our own mountain home. . . .

Little wonder that the leadership of the Church felt impelled to speak out against this sacrilegious, apostate deception by calling this wickedness to the attention of the members of the Church in a special item in the Church Priesthood Bulletin of August 1971.[125]

Dr. Reid Nibley, Professor of Music at Brigham Young University, believes that music tends to communicate the soul of the composer:

> The real test of music comes from the heart of the composer. Bach said that the aim and final reason of all music should be nothing else but the glory of God and the refreshment of the

spirit. Hayden even dressed in his best clothes to compose because he said he was going before his Maker. Beethoven was almost deaf when he composed his 9th Symphony which indicates his music was inspired by the Spirit. Brahms observed that an atheist could never be a great composer. "When I feel the urge to compose, I begin by appealing to my Maker. My desire and resolve is to be inspired so that I can compose something that will uplift and benefit humanity, something of permanent value."[126]

Rock Music

While many of the greatest classical musicians who ever lived claimed to be inspired of God, many of the "greats" and "pioneers" of rock music claim a different source of inspiration. Keith Richards of the Rolling Stones states: "The Stones' songs came spontaneously like an inspiration at a seance. The tunes arrived 'en masse' as if the Stones as songwriters were only a willing and open medium."[127] Yoko Ono, wife of Beatles member John Lennon, said of the group: "They were like mediums. They weren't conscious of all they were saying, but it was like coming through them."[128] Little Richard experienced similar influences, and identified Satan as the source of his inspiration: "I was directed and commanded by another power. The power of darkness . . . that a lot of people don't believe exists. The power of the Devil. Satan." He also gave his view of Rock music in general:

> My true belief about Rock 'n' Roll—and there have been a lot of phrases attributed to me over the years—is this: I believe this kind of music is demonic. . . . A lot of the beats in music today are taken from voodoo, from the voodoo drums. If you study music in rhythms, like I have, you'll see that it is true. . . .[129]

Jimi Hendrix believed he was possessed by some spirit. Hendrix's former girlfriend, Fayne Pridgon, said: "He used to always talk about some devil or something was in him, you know, and he didn't have any control over it, he didn't know what made him act the way he acted and what made him say the things he said, and songs . . . just came out of him. . . ."[130] Ozzy Osburn, a former member of Black Sabbath and popular Heavy Metal soloist, said: "I don't know if I'm a medium for some outside force or not. Frankly, whatever it is, I hope it's not what I think it is, Satan."[131] Peter Criss, formerly with the group KISS (Knights In Satan's Service) stated: "I believe in the devil as much as God. You can use either one to get things done."[132]

Rock Lyrics

Rock stars and their music can be dangerous enough when they are inspired by Satan, but when combined with the wrong kind of lyric, rock music can be spiritually deadly. Some lyrics are blatantly sexual or violent, while others are written in cryptic language as a door to occult teachings. Others are hidden entirely unless played backwards.

Whatever the lyrical form, parents should be aware of the dangerous messages transmitted in their children's music.

Composer Lex De Azevedo, an active Latter-day Saint with decades of experience in the popular music business, has remarked:

> The most striking example of the power of music occurs when words are added to the music. The music supplies the energy, power, and emotional impact, and the words give concrete ideas to music's abstract power. If the lyrics suggest evil, music is the sugar-coating on the pill that helps the bitter lyrics go down. We become so infatuated with the rhythm, the singer, the melody, that we translate this enduring emotion to the words, not caring what they really say. Whether the words are erotic, drug-oriented, violent, satanic, or just plain silly, when tied to a hit tune they sneak past the screening mechanism of the conscious mind to be stored in one's subconscious forever.[133]

In his book *The Satan-Seller*, Mike Warnke, a former Satanist, shows this demonic connection between Rock music, Satanism and drugs:

> I had planned on using acid rock to keep our young crowd tuned in . . . We had initiated hypnotic rock music as a prelude to our rituals and encourage heavier usage of drugs to get with it.[134]

John Todd claims that many rock lyrics are written in witch language by witches and you can't practice witchcraft without it. He claimed that Elton John had once declared that he had never written or sung a song that was not written in witch language. For example, Todd says, the lyrics to "Beyond the Yellow Brick Road," are in 100 percent witch language. This is why you don't understand many songs. They are supposed to only have meaning to those familiar with the occult—which makes these forms of rock a great proselyting tool among the youth. Witch language is also why many people don't understand certain songs until they get high on drugs: then the meanings suddenly start coming to them.

The Beatles "Double White" album is like a book of prophecy to witches, with nearly every song a prophecy, including the now infamous "Helter Skelter." Other songs like "Horse With No Name" and "One Tin Soldier" and thousands of other songs were written through satanic inspiration in language only understood by witches.[135]

It was reported in the *San Antonio Light*, on February 1, 1982, that backward-masked evil propaganda messages had been found in several groups' songs:

> Evil messages were not only found in the Beatles' music, but also in other rock groups, such as Led Zeppelin, Queen, Black Oak Arkansas and Electric Light Orchestra. This subliminal technique of hiding satanic messages is known as "Backward Masking." Messages that cannot be heard when played forward are implanted in the songs. This backward masking of messages can only be understood when the record is played backwards. . . . The Led Zeppelin song, "Stairway to Heaven," played backwards can be heard to say: *"MY SWEET SATAN."* . . . The Black Oak Arkansas song, "The Day Electricity Came to Arkansas," contains the backward message, *"SATAN, SATAN, SATAN, HE IS GOD."*[136]

Satanic messages can be placed into music by satanically inspired composers, even when the artist is unaware. Jeff Godwin, in his exposé on rock music, tells of an eerie Satanic prophecy on a record by one of the most anti-Christian artists of all time:

> Former *Beatle* John Lennon was shot to death in December, 1980. His "Double Fantasy" album had been in record stores for weeks. The song "Kiss, Kiss, Kiss" from that album contains a backmask [that sounds like Yoko Ono's voice] which says: *"WE SHOT JOHN LENNON."*
>
> If a demon didn't leave that little calling card, who did? How did Yoko Ono's human spirit KNOW, much less SAY, *"We Shot John Lennon,"* long before the murder happened? Mark David Chapman (Lennon's killer) admitted demonic spirits gave him the strength to carry out the execution.
>
> There's only one answer. That backmasked message on Lennon's record didn't come from a human spirit, it came from a demon's throat![137]

New Age Music

Randall N. Baer, formerly a world-renowned top New Age leader and author, converted to Christianity and traveled extensively to expose the deceptions of the New Age Movement. He had this to say of New Age music:

> New Age music has become a category unto itself. There is even a Grammy award category for this particular musical genre. In national record-seller chains, "New Age Music" warrants a distinct niche for itself. Thousands of New Age musicians vie for a widening national market with diverse musical styles. There are even New Age radio stations popping up in some of the major cities.
>
> However, not all that is generically categorized as New Age Music is necessarily demonic in nature. Though a significant chunk of music in this very generalized category is somewhat innocuous and entertaining, there is also a significant percent-

age in its ranks that promote and induce trance-states to higher consciousness. The repetitive, entrancing, floating quality of some of the New Age music genre can be potentially dangerous.

For myself, I feel it better to lean more towards the cautious and conservative side in discerning this realm of New Age Music.[138]

Just before Baer was to begin a series of television appearances to expose the deceptions of the New Age Movement, his car was found 330 feet down a cliff in a mountain area of Colorado. His death was termed "suspicious," as there were no skid marks at the top of the cliff.

The relaxing quality of New Age music has placed it in great demand. Whereas most rock music holds little appeal to older listeners and influences mainly the young, New Age Music with its relaxing meditative qualities can be more subtle in its influence.

While not all types of music or artists termed "New Age" are connected with the movement, a substantial portion are. To these artists, New Age music is as integral in setting the tone for New Age "worship" as hymns are for Christians. New Age music potentially poses a greater danger than rock music because it cuts across all age barriers and is becoming increasingly popular around the world. Former New Ager Elliot Miller discusses why this type of music is branded New Age:

> "New Age music" has roots in the New Age movement—the identical names are not a coincidence. The trend began with jazz luminaries like Paul Horn and John Fahey seeking to create music especially conductive to New Age spirituality. Then, as recounted by New Age seminar leader and entrepreneur Dick Sutphen, in the latter 1970s Steven Halpern created a "soothing music that was . . . great for visualizations. Structured on a pentatonic scale, there was no tension, no resolve, and it inspired without distracting" ("The Emergence of New Age Music" *Self-Help Update*, issue 29, 14). Halpern, who holds a master's degree in the psychology of music, was deliberately attempting

to facilitate the development of "higher" levels of consciousness.

This has remained a central goal for many New Age musicians to this day. Even Swiss harpist Andreas Vollenweider, whose records have sold in the millions, explains that the purpose of the tranquil sound is to "build a bridge between the conscious and the subconscious. We have to somehow excite our spirituality" (Bill Barol with Mark D. Uehling and George Raine, "Musak for a New Age," *Newsweek*, 13 May 1985, 68).[139]

Texe Marrs believes that New Age music, sometimes called "mood," "contemplative" and "meditative," can be "even more deadly to the spirit than heavy metal rock":

> New Age music is designed to bring the listener into a peaceful and hypnotic trance state during which demons can easily enter and take possession. It's been called "electronic meditation." A number of the New Age instrumentals have hidden subliminal messages. Supposedly, these messages can reprogram or rescript your brain.
>
> . . . New Age music can easily overwhelm the senses of young people and adults alike. Because it is more subtle and deceptive, it is even more harmful and deadly than any other form of music. . . .[140]

Concerning the intended rescripting of the brain, New Age composer Brother Charles told *Meditation* magazine: "I can open the doors of your (brain's) databanks. . . . As you're listening, the rescripting process is happening automatically via subliminally recorded messages."[141] Jeff Godwin says that the Christian music market is very gullible in its acceptance of the New Age meditation and subliminal tapes. He states that artists bury silent commands deep under layers of nature sounds in some of these titles, making this music New Age mind control at its worst:[142]

> The industry's premise is that we can recognize information presented below our threshold of awareness. Even though the

listener hears only soothing music or the sound of the ocean waves on an audio cassette or sees images of nature on a video, the subconscious mind can detect the hundreds or thousands of speeded-up, underlying subliminal suggestions, manufacturers say....[143]

If these subliminal messages cannot be consciously heard, how can one know what they are saying? Not even the companies who create these tapes will reveal this information. But there can be no doubt that manufacturers believe they can affect your behavior and thoughts subliminally. The text from the following advertisement demonstrates why all should be concerned:

> Subliminal messages are undetectable by the outer mind, yet easily picked up by the inner mind which influences many of our actions, habits, abilities, likes and dislikes. . . . You should play the tapes as often as possible but there is no need to 'consciously' listen to them. You simply turn on the tape and hear gentle ocean waves of music while you receive the desired messages without resistance from your outer mind. . . . You can be sure that 'extra care' has gone into preparing the content. For best results, use both sides of tape at least 30 times.
>
> The technical methods of recording the subliminal messages onto tapes are very critical. Reproduction is successful only when using special equipment. Therefore the positive effects are lost in attempting to make duplicates from a cassette.[144]

Godwin considers claims of special recording equipment to be "hogwash," because any sound that is recorded on one cassette can be transferred to another. What may not be transferred are spirit voices that were put on the original by spells of enchantment. "Too far out to believe? Satan would love for you to think so," he challenges.[145] While Godwin may not be able to prove his claim, hexes and spells are nevertheless an important characteristic in many branches of the New Age movement. It is not unreasonable to believe that a New Age-run organization would have someone cast spells on tapes so that they fulfill their advertising claims. If there is even the slightest possibility that this is happening, shouldn't such products be avoided at all costs?

Parents, if you notice an increase in rebellion in teenagers in the home it's probably your fault. You let your children listen to it. It stirs up rebellion. It's not so much the words in the song, it's the music. Witches know it. They hit certain chords on purpose.

Many people that have been involved in hypnosis can tell you the music is hypnotic. It stirs up a warlike nature in young people. You can either baby them because you're afraid they might get mad at you and run away from home, or you can go home and break the records and burn the covers.

All music has an effect on its listeners. The First Presidency and the Quorum of the Twelve have "reviewed, accepted and endorsed" the following guidelines concerning music in their summary of standards entitled "For the Strength of Youth":

> Music can help you draw closer to your Heavenly Father. It can be used to educate, edify, inspire, and unite. However, music may be used for wicked purposes. Music can, by its tempo, beat, intensity, and lyrics, dull your spiritual sensitivity. You cannot afford to fill your minds with unworthy music. Music is an important and powerful part of life. You must consider your listening habits thoughtfully and prayerfully. You should be willing to control your listening habits and shun music that is spiritually harmful. Don't listen to music that contains ideas that contradict principles of the gospel. Don't listen to music that promotes Satanism or other evil practices, encourages immorality, uses foul and offensive language, or drives away the Spirit. Use careful judgment and maturity to choose the music you listen to and the level of its volume.[146]

To those who attend functions where various forms of popular music are played, such as dance clubs, school dances and private parties, these guidelines, also set forth by the church in its standards pamphlet, should be followed:

Plan and attend dances where dress, grooming, lighting, dancing styles, lyrics, and music contribute to an atmosphere in which the Spirit of the Lord may be present.[147]

These standards, although specifically written for the youth, are just as applicable to all members of the Church and reinforce the need for caution in all that is listened to.

Chapter Seven

A NEW BIBLE PLANNED FOR MANKIND

The scriptures have warned that this would be a day of false Christs, false prophets, false miracles, false religions, false doctrines and false philosophies. Satan's counterfeit religions, prophets and apostles have always arisen to oppose the truth and deceive the Saints *(Joseph Smith 1:22, Revelation 13:13-14).*[148] This time, the machinery is veiled under the massive umbrella of the New Age Movement.

Previously, when Satan was successful in perverting the doctrines of Christ, the Western World experienced the unenlightening Dark Ages. All religious knowledge was restricted to the hands of a few elite and privileged priests. They in turn gave the uneducated masses the guidance which they felt the people needed. The Dark Ages were the last time Satan successfully restricted the flow of knowledge and true spiritual enlightenment from God on a global scale. It was an era ruled by degeneracy, destruction and stagnation of the mind. Superstition, murder and mayhem reigned supreme throughout the entire earth.

To achieve this type of New Age world again, Satan is using both his knowing followers and those who are deceived to implement a new way of thinking—one without any Christian moral restraints or beliefs. In his plan, revelation from God will have no place in this new, "liberated" society. Guidance will instead come from spiritualistic, intuitive, mystical and occult sources. The distinction between good and evil will be completely neutralized, and the divinity of Jesus Christ will be rationalized away. Man will be told that Christ was just an advanced teacher of hidden mysteries, and that he has advanced to another life state.

To support these so-called advancements, New Agers declare that hidden writings will be discovered, revealing new interpretations of the scriptures. Ancient words and terms will be assigned new meanings.

Even now, articles are beginning to appear in which biblical scholars claim they have found some "lost sermons" of Jesus which they believe to be in his own handwriting. These texts supposedly confirm that Jesus preached the doctrine of reincarnation to his disciples, that "death is not the end of one life but the beginning of another." They also explain that "even Satan may yet regain heaven, for the Father is merciful and has given the evil one the same destiny as man." The citizens of this New Age society will be told that these New Scriptures can be changed whenever new discoveries warrant revisions.[149]

This author has correlated some of the changes from the King James Version of the Bible which appear in several different Bible versions. University professor and Christian Bible researcher G. A. Riplinger made the following observations about these changes:[150]

> Oriental mystics, traveling West via the New Age Movement, are adopting Christian Terms for their occult ideas and identities. . . . So now 'Buddha', 'Krishna', and Lucifer become 'The Lord', 'The Christ', and 'the One'. Occult initiation becomes 'baptism', the beginning step on their 'Way'.
>
> . . . The new versions [of the Bible] give a picture of the widening apostasy. And like a photographic negative, it is a dim view. When held up to the light of God's word, it is clearly discernible that they are pictures of the coming One World Religion.[151]

The following are some examples of these changes that have been made in various modern versions of the Bible. Note how they move away from declaring the supremacy of the Father and The Son and the degeneracy of Lucifer.

Isaiah 14:12

King James Version - How art thou fallen from heaven, O *Lucifer*, son of the morning! . . .

New International Version - How you have fallen from heaven, O *morning star*, son of the dawn! . . .

American Standard Bible - How art thou fallen from heaven, O *day-star*, son of the morning! . . .

Revised Standard Version - How you are fallen from heaven, O *Day Star*, son of Dawn! . . .

Notice how the name *Lucifer* has been completely removed.

Luke 4:8

KJV - And Jesus answered and said unto him, *Get thee behind me, Satan:* for it is written, Thou shalt worship the Lord thy God, and him only shalt thou serve.

NIB - Jesus answered, "It is written: 'Worship the Lord your God and serve him only.'"

ASB - And Jesus answered and said unto him, It is written, Thou shalt worship the Lord thy God, and him only shalt thou serve.

RSV - And Jesus answered him, "It is written, 'You shall worship the Lord your God, and him only shall you serve.'"

As you can see, the phrase *"Get thee behind me, Satan"* has been completely removed.

Romans 1:20

KJV - For the invisible things of him from the creation of the world are clearly seen, being understood by the things that are made, even his eternal power and *Godhead*; so that they are without excuse:

NIB - For since the creation of the world God's invisible qualities—his eternal power and *divine nature*—have been clearly seen, being understood from what has been made, so that men are without excuse.

ASB - For the invisible things of him since the creation of the world are clearly seen, being perceived through the things that are made, even his everlasting power and *divinity*; that they may be without excuse:

RSV - Ever since the creation on the world his invisible nature, namely, his eternal power and *deity*, has been clearly perceived in the things that have been made. So they are without excuse;

In this verse all reference to the *Godhead* has been deleted.

Ephesians 3:14

KJV - For this cause I bow my knees unto the *Father of our Lord Jesus Christ,*

NIB - For this reason I kneel before the *Father,*

ASB - For this cause I bow my knees unto the *Father,*

RSV - For this reason I bow my knees before the *Father,*

All mention of Jesus Christ has been totally eliminated from this verse.

Mark 12:32

KJV - And the scribe said unto him, Well, Master, thou hast said the truth: for there is one *God* and there is none other but he:

NIB - "Well said, *teacher,*" the man replied. "You are right in saying that *God is One* and there is no other but him.

ASB - And the scribe said unto him, of a truth, *Teacher*, thou hast well said that *he is one*; and there is none other but he:

RSV - And the scribe said to him, "You are right, *Teacher*: you have truly said that *he is one*, and there is no other but he;

In this verse the reference to *"one God"* has been changed to *"he is one."*

John 6:69

KJV - And we believe and are sure that thou art *that Christ, the Son of the living God.*

NIB - We believe and know that you are *the Holy One of God.*

ASB - And we have believed and know that thou art *the Holy One of God.*

RSV - and we have believed, and have come to know, that you are *the Holy One of God.*

Although just a few of the many Bible comparisons made are shown here, it is enough to see that the Bible is being changed and corrupted.

If these changes seem to make little difference to Christians, they are significant to the New Age. *In the preceding versions of the Bible the term "Holy One" is not interpreted by the New Age to mean "Jesus Christ."* Occultist and Luciferian Madame Blavatsky openly declares in her book The *Secret Doctrine* that *'the One'* is not Jehovah and that this *'One' claims* he is superior to Eloheim. (Doesn't that sound like the same arrogance Lucifer exhibited before he was cast out of heaven by the forces of Jehovah and Michael?) Blavatsky lists other names 'the One' is known by: The Dragon of Wisdom, the Dragon, Lucifer, Satan, The Fiery Serpent, Hermes, Sat, Pan, Kumara, the Mysterious One, and the Devil, to name a few They are all the same personage,[152] that same egotistical and insolent son of the morning that held high esteem, rank, honor and authority in the first estate before he rebelled and was "thrust down" (see D & C 76:25-28).

The "Jesus" that many New Agers believe in, according to New Age thought, gained the office of "the Christ" only after he was purified and progressed through several reincarnations. They believe he is but one of several "masters" from a higher plane, although not the highest.

New Age Holistic Health

The New Age aggressively has moved into the area of Holistic health because of the groundswell of disillusionment with the orthodox medical establishment. Former New Ager Randall Baer completed a two-year course of study leading to an N.D. (naturopathic doctor). He explained the difficulties encountered when trying to analyze what is and is not New Age in the holistic health field:

> Holistic medicine is one of the trickiest areas to sort out the New Age from the non-New Age. This is to say, a holistic professional might recommend that a person do aerobic exercise and take a multi-vitamin, but doing the exercise and taking the vitamin is not necessarily New Age. This important issue of discerning and separating what is and is not New Age in the field of holistic health is often a complex and subtle one requiring extensive examination.
>
> . . . The essential problem is that New Age philosophy lies at the core of much of the holistic health field. . . .
>
> The area of holistic health is one of the most subtle and sophisticated areas of the murky merging of the esoteric and the mundane, the metaphysical with the mainstream, the pseudo-scientific with the scientific, the non-New Age with the New Age.[153]

This is an area in which the discerning power of the Holy Ghost is needed. Some techniques are so openly satanic that they can be spotted right away. Others are more subtle, initially sounding like a rational scientific discovery. Be alert and careful: a mistake can lead one down strange paths and into encounters with dangerous spiritual forces. (Before illustrating the problem, let it first be said that this author believes in the individual's right to choose which remedies he wants. The government should not restrict free choice in the health field except in cases of outright fraud.)

However, many unproven and dangerous practices are labeled as remedies, such as the new mystical "hand-motion treatment" sensation sweeping through the nursing profession called "Therapeutic Touch." This "treatment" claims tens of thousands of practitioners throughout the world. Practitioners move their hands a few inches away from a seated patient's body, soothing kinks or congestion in the "energy field" that supposedly surrounds all humans. They claim to relax patients, relieve pain, and cause chemical changes in the blood to promote healing.[154]

Great care must be taken in this type of practice as many are essentially practicing a type of "laying on of hands." Many things are not the beneficial practices they first seem to be, nor what they purport to be in their promotional materials. New Age magazines promote these holistic practices as readily as they do healing by crystals, Eastern mystic yoga practices, subliminal tapes, New Age music composed in trance, medicine men, magic jewelry, psychic healing, and many other means too numerous to mention.

Hidden New Age Seminars

Self-improvement, stress-reduction and consciousness-expanding seminars are ideal vehicles for New Age adherents to promote their dogma. These psychological programs often integrate deceptively Satanic practices. Robyn Brown, an LDS housewife from California, explained in *The Ensign* how these teachings can subvert gospel principles:

> All my life I have searched to find the happiness that the scriptures promise we can enjoy on this earth. I always expected happiness to come from an outside source. I mistakenly felt that when I lost a few pounds, or got married, or had children, or owned my own home, I would then be happy.
>
> As the years passed, I felt that I was missing out on the abundant life the Savior promised us. I continued to search for a magic formula that would make me happy.

Not long ago, I was introduced to a private self-improvement seminar that promised to *expand my consciousness and help me achieve all my goals in life.* The classes were initially organized and taught by people who professed to be members of the Church, so I felt comfortable and safe enrolling in them.

The first course consisted of nearly fifty hours of instruction packed into a single, intense week. All my expectations seemed to be fulfilled. Gospel truths were used to help us see ourselves in a better, more complete light. Emotional pain seemed to melt away through the instruction, group role-playing, and psychological tactics employed.

I was so elated by the "progress" I was making that I enrolled in the second phase of the course. But then the direction and focus of the course subtly changed. I was taught concepts that seemed contrary to the teachings of Jesus Christ. I was led to believe that it was my own lack of understanding that caused me to question these strange new ideas.

One of the falsehoods subtly interjected was that there is no need to strive for perfection or even to be concerned about our own destiny. We were taught that everyone is on his or her perfect path and that, no matter what he did in mortality, we would all achieve the celestial kingdom. Even Satan and his followers, we were told, would be there.

Perhaps most disturbing was that I was specifically counseled not to tell my husband what I had learned. Spouses could never understand the new concepts being taught, the instructor said, until they had taken the first course.

I had always shared my feelings with my husband, and I told him about what I had learned. *He tried to show me how the courses had programmed me to accept false teachings—they had the effect of brainwashing.*

I thought I could prove him wrong. My husband prayed and fasted, then asked me to go to the temple with him. I agreed to go. We sat in the celestial room and talked, and the spirit of the Lord let me know how wrong I was.

When we returned home, I could feel the adversary's presence. He had nearly misdirected me, and he knew he was losing me. I read the scriptures until I finally felt his presence leave.

Though the experience of having my testimony challenged was very painful for me, it also initiated great personal growth. I have come to realize more fully that, as Nephi taught, I must not put my trust in the arm of flesh (see 2 Nephi 4:34), but must rely instead on the teachings of the Savior.

I now understand that there are no quick remedies for life's problems and frustrations. True and lasting happiness comes only by following the teachings of the Savior and his servants, the prophets. (Emphasis added.)[155]

Spiritualism, Witchcraft and Astrology

The Old Testament tells about some of the forms of mysticism which existed, of which man should beware:

> Regard not them that have familiar spirits, neither seek after wizards, to be defiled by them: (Leviticus 19:31).

Also,

> There shall not be found among you any one that maketh his son or his daughter to pass through the fire, or that useth divination, or an observer of times, or an enchanter, or a witch,
>
> Or a charmer, or a consulter with familiar spirits, or a wizard, or a necromancer (Deuteronomy 18:10-11).

Elder Bruce R. McConkie gives definitions and explanations of what these terms and others being used today really mean:

> ASTROLOGY: A form of divination and fortune telling akin to sorcery, *astrology* is a pseudo science that pretends to divulge the influence of the stars upon human affairs; . . . It is, of course, one of Satan's substitutes for the true science of astronomy . . .

DIVINATION: . . . This practice is an attempt to foretell the future by auguries, omens, presages, or forebodings. . . .

NECROMANCY: *Necromancy* is that form of divination which attempts to foretell the future by consultation with the dead. Sometimes the term is enlarged to include magic in general. . . .

OCCULTISM: *Occultism* has reference to the hidden and mysterious powers subject to the control of those who engage in divination, alchemy, astrology, sorcery, and magic. . . .

SPIRITUALISM: Those religionists who attempt and frequently attain communion (as they suppose) with departed spirits are called *spiritualists*. . . . Such communion, if and when it occurs, is manifest by means of physical phenomena, such as so-called spirit-rappings, or during abnormal mental states, such as in trances. . . .

WITCHCRAFT: One of the most evil and wicked sects supported by Satan is that which practices witchcraft, such craft involving as it does actual intercourse with evil spirits. A *witch* is one who engages in this craft, who practices the black art of magic, who has entered into a compact with Satan, who is a sorcerer or sorceress. . . .[156]

Astrology and Spiritualism

The cornerstone of spiritualism and witchcraft is astrology. Ex Grand Druid witchcraft leader John Todd stated that you "cannot cast a spell, you cannot mix a potion, you cannot do a rite without a firm knowledge of astrology. It is the basis for all practices in witchcraft."[157]

One of astrology's teachings is that one is born with a set personality and there is nothing he or she can do to change. This paganistic philosophy claims to interpret the will of the star Gods. William Josiah Sutton explains astrology's key role in the New Age deceptions:

> The chief star gods of the pagans were the gods of Astrology, which were believed to be just emanations of the one god, the Sun-god, the ruler of the Zodiac. Astrology is the foundation of all the pagan sciences of the occult, whose author is Lucifer, and his spirit guides are his angels. Spiritualism, which is just another name for Witchcraft, is today among the young, the biggest rival of Jesus Christ. It will be through Spiritualism that men and women will come with all manner of lying wonders that will gather the whole world under Satan's banner. . . .
>
> Spiritualism (Witchcraft) will deceive the whole world into accepting a strong delusion that will bring Satan to finally use his crowning deception that will cause most to lose their salvation. Lucifer, the Old Serpent, called the Devil, will impersonate Jesus Christ just before the real Christ comes the Second Time. This will be Satan's last effort to destroy mankind. However, students of the Bible, who have made Scripture the only standard to judge between truth and error, will not be fooled into worshipping Satan as Christ. For the satanic movement to unite the world under one banner and Christ walking upon this earth again is a complete contradiction of Scripture. . . .[158]

Sutton continues and clarifies the relationship of Spiritualism and Astrology to the New Age Movement and the coming anti-Christ:

> Astrology teaches that the human race will pass through seven ages. Before each age a Christ, according to Spiritualism, was to appear to usher in each New Age. We live in the Age of Pisces, 0-2000 AD, and according to Spiritualism we are about to enter into the "Age of Aquarius," which will begin in the year 2000 AD. Whether or not this is the long awaited appearance of the Antichrist foretold from Scripture still remains to be seen. For there *"are many antichrists."* 1 John 2:18. The Devil himself will appear as Jesus Christ just before the real Jesus of Nazareth appears in the heavens. II Thessalonians 2:3-11. Satan will [im]personate Jesus as He is described in Revelation 1: 13-15. This false Christ Maitreya, according to [a] newspaper article, will appear as an ordinary modern man.[159]

It is the spread of Spiritualism around the world that will ultimately make the appearance of the anti-Christ described in Revelation possible. Satan knows his time is short, so his final big push before the Savior returns is well underway. He will deceive and destroy as much of mankind as he can before that day arrives. The Lord has warned of this danger.[160]

Former New Age leader Randall Baer, while in a self-induced mystical out-of-body experience, discovered the duplicity and deception in these spiritualistic practices and how Satan deceives by counterfeiting light and truth:

> . . . the ultimate seduction had overtaken me: What I thought was "up" was actually "down." What I thought was "heaven" was actually "hell" wrapped in Satan's finest counterfeit garments. What I thought were Ascended Masters, extraterrestrials, and angels were actually demons in cunning, glowing disguises.
>
> . . . Darkness can have an outer covering, so to speak, of luminosity that can appear to be inexpressibly beautiful. The power of darkness can feel wonderfully beauteous, too. Satan and his demonic legions are masterful counterfeiters who can make darkness appear to be light, untruth appear to be truth and hate appear to be love. The luminosity of darkness can be so bright that it bedazzles to the point of blindness and mesmerizes to the point of brainwashing. This is exactly what happened to me, and what is happening today to all those involved in the New Age Movement.
>
> One night, while in the Ascension Chamber, my spirit was roaming some of the farthest reaches of "heavenly light" that I had ever perceived. That night I had an experience that would change my life forever.
>
> During this experience I was surrounded by a virtually overwhelming luminosity—it was as if I was looking straight into the sun. Waves of bliss radiated through my spirit. I was totally captivated by the power.

Suddenly, another force stepped in. It took me by complete surprise. In the twinkling of an eye, it was like a supernatural hand had taken me behind the scenes of the experience that I was having. I was taken behind the outer covering of the dazzling luminosity and there saw something that left me literally shaking for a full week.

What I saw was the face of devouring darkness! Behind the glittering outer facade of beauty lay a massively powerful, wildly churning face of absolute hatred and unspeakable abominations—the face of demons filled with the power of Satan.

For a moment that seemed like an eternity, I realized that I was in major league trouble, for this devouring force was now closing in on me.

In absolute, stark terror I felt powerless to stop what appeared to be inevitable doom. Horror filled me like a consuming flame.

Then, miraculously, the same supernatural hand as before delivered me from the jaws of this consuming darkness. . . .

What I didn't know at the time was that it was JESUS who had intervened by His greater grace into my life. At this point, though, I only knew that some force greater than that of the devouring darkness had done two things: 1) it had shown me the real face of the New Age "heavens" and "angels" that I was so deeply involved with, and 2) it had delivered me from certain doom.[161]

Elder John A. Widtsoe explains how Satan, the author of Spiritualism, and his agents imitate and counterfeit the truth in order to deceive and destroy mankind:

Satan also has his messengers. The hosts who fell from heaven in the preexistent council are busily engaged in opposition to God's purposes for man's salvation. They are sent out to lead men into sin. They are angels of untruth, therefore of evil. They feed on lies.

These evil "angels" use deception as their main tool of destruction. They simulate all that is good. They urge the satisfaction of sensual appetites. In the words of Brigham Young, they tell a hundred truths so that the one lie may be accepted. Sometimes they may come as angels of light, in borrowed or stolen raiment. Always they fail to reveal themselves as they are.[162]

Satan will inspire the wicked to anger against God and stir them up with all kinds of deceptions, lies and flatteries. However, the Lord will hold those who seek to destroy his work accountable for their actions. Even though Satan is the driving force seeking to destroy the souls of men, men still have the agency to reject or follow his enticements. They will not be able to use deception as an excuse to be exempt from the justice of God (*D & C 10:12, 23-29; 93:31-32*). It is the responsibility of the Saints to fight evil wherever it may be.

Chapter Eight

WHO IS LORD MAITREYA?

In April 1982 The Tara Center, headed by New Ager Benjamin Creme, declared in full-page ads in a number of leading newspapers that the true Messiah—a combination of Jewish Messiah, Christian Jesus Christ, Muslim Mahdi, Hindu Krishna and the Buddhist Lord Maitreya all rolled into one—*was already alive and well, living somewhere in east London.* Creme purports that *Maitreya has been in London since 1977.*[163]

Latter-day Saints would be wise to learn more about this so-called New Age "messiah," Lord Maitreya. Is he possessed? Is he the anti-Christ? How and when will he present himself to the public? The following is a reproduction of the copy from an ad that was placed in the *Los Angeles Times* to herald the coming of a great world teacher that is supposedly going to bring peace and justice to all humanity:

On April 25, 1982, many people were simultaneously startled by full-page ads that were placed in key newspapers around the world proclaiming that "The Christ Is Now Here."

These ads said that he was a modern man concerned with modern political, economic and social problems, and will be recognized by his *"extraordinary spiritual potency."* In other words, he will exhibit an *unnatural* and spellbinding (satanic) spiritual power and influence. He is the head of a "Spiritual Hierarchy" and is known as Lord Maitreya:

THE WORLD HAS HAD *enough* ...
OF HUNGER, INJUSTICE, WAR.
IN ANSWER TO OUR CALL, FOR HELP, AS WORLD
TEACHER FOR ALL HUMANITY,

THE CHRIST IS NOW HERE.

HOW WILL WE RECOGNIZE HIM?

Look for a modern man concerned with modern problems - political, economic, and social. Since July, 1977, the Christ has been emerging as a spokesman for a group or community in a well-known modern country. He is not a religious leader, but an educator in the broadest sense of the word—pointing the way out of our present crisis. We will recognize Him by His extraordinary spiritual potency, the universality of His viewpoint, and His love for all humanity. He comes not to judge, but to aid and inspire.

WHO IS THE CHRIST?

Throughout history, humanity's evolution has been guided by a group of enlightened men, the Masters of Wisdom. They have remained largely in the remote desert and mountain places of earth, working mainly through their disciples who live openly in the world. This message of the Christ's reappearance has been given primarily by such a disciple trained for his task for over twenty years. At the center of this "Spiritual Hierarchy" stands the World Teacher, *Lord Maitreya,* known by Christians as the *Christ*. And as Christians await the Second Coming, so the Jews await the *Messiah*, the Buddhists the fifth *Buddha*, the Moslems *Imn Mahdi*, and the Hindus await *Krishna*.

These are all names for one individual.

His presence in the world guarantees there will be no third World War.

WHAT IS HE SAYING?

"My task will be to show you how to live together peacefully as brothers. This is simpler than you imagine, My friends, for it requires only the acceptance of sharing."

"How can you be content with the modes within which you now live: when millions starve and die in squalor; when the rich

parade their wealth before the poor; when each man is his neighbor's enemy; when no man trusts his brother? "Allow me to show you the way forward into a simpler life where no man lacks; where no two days are alike; where the Joy of Brotherhood manifests through all men."

"Take your brother's need as the measure for your action and solve the problems of the world."

WHEN WILL WE SEE HIM?

He has not as yet declared His true status, and His location is known to only a very few disciples. One of these has announced that soon the Christ will acknowledge His identity and within the next two months will speak to humanity through a worldwide television and radio broadcast. His message will be heard inwardly, telepathically, by all people in their own language. From that time, with His help,
we will build a new world.

WITHOUT SHARING THERE CAN BE NO JUSTICE;
WITHOUT JUSTICE THERE CAN BE NO PEACE;
WITHOUT PEACE THERE CAN BE NO FUTURE.

This statement is appearing simultaneously in
major cities of the world.

INFORMATION CENTER AMSTERDAM
P.O. BOX 41877
1009 DB AMSTERDAM
HOLLAND

THE TARA PRESS
59 DARTMOUTH PARK ROAD
LONDON NW5 1SL
ENGLAND

TARA CENTER
90 UNIVERSITY PL.
NEW YORK, N.Y. 10003
U.S.A.

TARA CENTER
P.O. BOX 6001
N. HOLLYWOOD, CA 91603
U.S.A.[164]

Lord Maitreya is referred to as the coming "Christ" by many New Age groups. In order to deflect criticism, many refrain from naming him and use general titles such as "the enlightened one to come," the "Cosmic Christ," the "Universal One," or the "New Age World Teacher" instead in referring to him.[165] The word 'Maitreya' is from the sacred language of the Hindus, Sanskrit, and it means 'Merciful One.' According to Creme, Maitreya is the Christ, Head of our planetary Hierarchy.

Dr. J. Gordon Melton, a religious historian who has watched Benjamin Creme's odyssey, wrote:

> During the 1970s, according to Creme, Maitreya materialized a human body into which he incarnated. In 1977 he flew from Karachi to London and took up residence in the Indian-Pakistani community in London where he began to speak regularly to audiences numbered in the hundreds. On April 24-25, 1982, through advertisements taken out in a number of the world's prominent newspapers, Creme announced that Maitreya's "Day of Declaration" would occur within two months. Followers expected it on or before June 21, 1982. When the Declaration failed to occur and Maitreya failed to appear, Creme blamed the apathy of the media (a sign of general human apathy). He also announced that the Day of Declaration was still imminent though no new specific date was set. In the meantime, the followers were urged to continue their main task of announcing that Christ is in the world and soon to appear.[166]

Benjamin Creme said that Maitreya will only reveal himself when he feels mankind is ready. Creme says he will eliminate strife and disease, and he said that a New Age will be ushered in with love, peace and shared wealth. He also is aware that Christian fundamentalists view Maitreya as either the anti-Christ prophesied in the Bible, or as someone much like him. Constance Cumby explains the true nature of this anti-Christ:

When Benjamin Creme, spokesman for the so-called Maitreya the Christ, spoke in Detroit on November 4, 1981, he was asked if he had ever met the Christ. His answer was revealing. He said, "No, I've never met the Christ, but I've met the human body he is inhabiting several times—but never as the Christ." This reveals the real nature of the Antichrist and the power behind the New Age movement in general. It constitutes nothing less than old-fashioned demonic possession. The person who will eventually be the Antichrist and consequently the chief spokesman for Satan will be an adult who freely and voluntarily decided to assume the spirit of Satan.[167]

Creme has explained away Christ's role as the redeemer of mankind, relegating him to the role of only being a religious leader, like Buddha or the Krishna. Creme explains that Jesus of Nazareth was just a disciple of Maitreya's and that he was only a temporary Christ who was initiated into Maitreya's hierarchy as a Senior Master. Christ has reincarnated and currently lives in Rome, Creme says. Just to set the record straight, Maitreya says that Jesus was not Jewish, that he was not from the ancestry of David, and he was not born of a virgin.

Maitreya says that all mankind will be introduced to the ancient mysteries and that the new seat of world government will be the United Nations.[168]

Monte Leach, the United States editor of Share International journal, in an interview with *The New American* at the International Development Conference in Washington, D.C. said:

> ... The "Master of all the Masters and Teacher alike of angels and men" is alive and among men today.
> ... Leach is a disciple of Benjamin Creme, the British Theosophist who speaks on behalf of "Lord Maitreya," an enigmatic ersatz messiah who resides in the Indian quarter of London.
> ... Leach states that "what most people don't realize is that behind the scenes, for thousands and thousands of years, the

Great Teachers have been guiding humanity, helping it take the next step in its development."

The "Masters" intervene in human affairs by overshadowing individuals, [possession of] according to Leach, and such "overshadowings" have been common in mankind's past.

. . . "Now, for the first time in thousands of years, the Masters are returning to work openly among humanity" . . . *Not since the Atlantean era in pre-history has such a thing happened. In a way it's unprecedented.*

. . . Furthermore, the "Masters" are reportedly prepared to create the "New World Religion and Universal Church." The December 1994 *Share International* contains an essay by Aart Jurriaase, a South African disciple of Alice Bailey, entitled "The New World Religion." Jurriaase writes that "the One Church and the New World Religion . . . will gradually emerge as a mutual tie to untie men with closer bonds. This great objective of eventually gathering all peoples of the world into the one great Universal Church, is the task of the Masters Coot Homo and Moray, assisted by the Master Jesus [as the Theosophists understand him]."

. . . Every issue of *Share International* includes a message from "The Master," who is identified as "a senior member of the Hierarchy of the Masters of Wisdom. . . . "The Master" issues edicts to the world regarding spiritual affairs. The Message contained in the December issue is entitled "He awaits your recognition." According to "The Master," "Very soon now, a most unusual event will allow the world to know that the Masters do, indeed exist. . . . "That revelation will impose a stark choice on mankind, as this somewhat ominous passage suggests: "When men see Maitreya, they will know that the time has come to choose: to go forward with Him into a future dazzling in its promise—or to cease to be." Whoever Creme's "Master" may be, his ultimatum is not a pronouncement inspired by the biblical Prince of Peace.[169]

The New Age movement is teaching that we are on the verge of a major event in history. They believe that this Great World teacher will lead mankind into a One World Order along with a new One World Religion that will bring peace and prosperity throughout the world. However, there needs to be some extreme world crisis that will make the world clamor for a leader who will guide the world out of its emergency and save it from the brink of destruction. This great world leader will undoubtedly be a very charismatic individual endowed with great persuasive powers, charm and diplomacy. So great will be his influence, ability and prestige that throughout the world the leaders will rally behind him with their confidence and support so he can solve the world's ills. What most New Ager's do not know is that they will ultimately be betrayed by him and brought under the same oppression as the rest of the world.

Most Christians, however, are fully aware that a powerful leader/deceiver will rule before the second coming of the Savior, one who will be known as an anti-Christ and man of deceit. He will wield extreme influence, power and authority and it will be "given unto him to make war with the saints, and to overcome them: and power was given him over all kindreds, and tongues, and nations" *(Revelation 13:7)*. He will overcome the saints temporally for a period, but not spiritually.

He will become so powerful and arrogant and wrapped up in his own power, strength and self-importance that he will open "his mouth in blasphemy against God, to blaspheme his name, and his tabernacle, and them that dwell in heaven" *(Revelation 13:6)*.

This type of arrogant display will take on a violent nature when some people refuse to take the satanic initiation and mark of allegiance to him and his organization. His rage will have no bounds. Understanding that this mark will signify allegiance to Satan through initiation gives a much clearer perception of the mark's seriousness. That's why angels delivered these admonitions and warnings to the Saints:

> . . . Fear God, and give glory to him; for the hour of his judgment is come: . . . If any man worship the beast and his image, and receive his mark in his forehead, or in his hand,

> The same shall drink of the wine of the wrath of God, which is poured out without mixture into the cup of his indignation; and he shall be tormented with fire and brimstone in the presence of the holy angels, and in the presence of the Lamb:
>
> And the smoke of their torment ascendeth up for ever and ever: and they have no rest day or night, who worship the beast and his image, and whosoever receiveth the mark of his name (Revelation 14:7, 9-11).

The New World Order desired by the Illuminati and many of the world's leaders might well be the fulfillment of the prophecies in Revelation 13. This chapter tells of the coming forth of this secretive and powerful kingdom to arise and to hold great power, authority and satanic influence in the latter-days under the direction of Satan and a great world leader. This great deceiver of mankind will command and dominate a world economy, a world government, and a world religion (Revelation 13:4-17). When this anti-Christ emerges to take the reigns of world government there will already be in place an occult New Age army of millions around the world who are predisposed, prepared and willing to receive and embrace his leadership as the only hope for mankind. Many of this following will have been organized under the umbrella of the New Age Movement.

The Year 2000 and the Age of Aquarius

Many of these same world leaders are planning another great event or celebration that will mark the dawning of the New Age of Aquarius which officially begins in the year 2000. It is a very special year and new beginning for the Illuminati, for the New Age Movement, and for many occultists. They are planning a special victory party for their New Age leadership. It was reported in The National Educator that on October 19, 1989 scientists from the top secret Nellis Atomic Test Site (area 51) in Nevada launched:

> ... The Galileo Space Probe to explore the planet Jupiter. It left Earth with $49\frac{1}{4}$ pounds of plutonium which is used for

nuclear fission. The Galileo mission is to reach the planet by 1995, circle it for four and a half years, and then be drawn into its ignitable atmosphere—*by the year 2000*. The Age of Aquarius.

Could it be a coincidence that the current September 1992 issue of Life Magazine's latest article on their NASA/SETI feature is authored by Arthur C. Clarke? In Clarke's book, '2010: Space Odyssey,' he describes in the last page of the last chapter our Earth having a binary star system as a result of the intellectual elite having sent a space probe to the planet Jupiter which would ignite the planet's atmosphere, thus [illuminating] the night with light. The planet is to be renamed Lucifer, 'Bearer of the Light.'[170]

Texe Marrs has this to say regarding the year 2000 and this deceptive New Age burst of radiance:

> Masons and other Sun God worshipping secret societies measure calendar years beginning in the year 4000 B.C. The year 1999 is therefore 5999 AL (AL stands for "Anno Lucis," in the year of light"). In 6000 AL (2000 AD) the dawning of the *New Millennium*, the long awaited New Age, is to burst into radiance, transforming the whole world. The dominance of Lucifer, known by the occultists as the "Light Bearer," the bright morning star, shall then come into full being.[171]

Aric Z. Leavitt, in his private publication titled simply *The Illuminati*, adds these details:

> At the end of the year 1999 A.D., there will be a party held at the base of the Great Pyramid in Egypt. This celebration will coincide with the dawning of the New Aquarian Age, or, what is simply known to us as the 21st Century. In attendance at this historical party hosted by the Illuminati, through the Millennium Society, will be every living past President of the United States . . . and no doubt the current one, whatever he'll be called, since by that time this country would not technically

exist anymore. We can only wonder if they'll be in their black robes, which they wear at their party sessions in the Bohemian Grove. In a sense, this planned future event will be a way for these men in their arrogance to let the world know they were in on it all along. They knew what they were doing. Conspiracy confirmed! And if they do, in fact, hold to their schedule, in conjunction with phase three of the Galileo mission and the rise of "DAYSTAR," we'll hear the ultimate blasphemy: a proclamation that "Lucifer is God!"

. . . If the new generation does not prepare for the war at hand, it will otherwise prepare for death. It can either "mount up with wings as eagles" or "stay the course." A nation that worships false gods will inevitably crash out of history. America's idolatry, outside of religious apostasy, takes the form of a frantic search for pleasure that never satisfies.[172]

It is very interesting to note that George Bush publicly stated his intention to be present in Egypt at the Great Pyramid on December 31, 1999 at the stroke of midnight to welcome in the New Millennium.[173]

Whatever it is these individuals are up to, it doesn't sound like it's going to be of any benefit to the general public. Remember, New Agers want to cleanse the world of some two billion people before the year 2000.[174]

Chapter Nine

WHAT IS THE RESPONSIBILITY OF THE SAINTS?

Many Saints have rationalized that if it were their responsibility to actively recognize and fight specific dangers, the general authorities would inaugurate a church-wide program, via official priesthood channels, with specific instructions on how to proceed. Many believe they have no responsibility outside their immediate sphere of influence, hoping that if they faithfully attend all their church meetings and study gospel principles, that the Lord will solve all the world's problems without their help.

Such are "at ease in Zion" (2 Nephi 28:24), a dangerous condition that comes from not understanding the ways of the Lord. Elder Dallin H. Oaks of the Quorum of the Twelve Apostles explains that the general authorities cannot possibly champion every righteous cause, or speak the political jargon of the day:

> A desire to be lead by the Lord is a strength, but it needs to be accompanied by an understanding that our Heavenly Father leaves many decisions for our personal choices. Personal decision making is one of the sources of the growth we are meant to experience in mortality. . . .
>
> We should study things out in our minds, using the reasoning powers our creator has placed within us. Then we should pray for guidance and act upon it if we receive it. If we do not receive guidance, we should act upon our best judgment.[175]

While one may not hear the words "New Age" from the pulpit, the Saints are constantly admonished to resist what turns out to be the defining principles of the New Age: worship of self, moral relativism, reliance on the arm of flesh, immorality, dissolution of the family, false doctrines, lack of faith in Christ, pride, spiritualism, sin and blasphemy.

Likewise, the Saints have been instructed that the basic unit of government is the family (not any government institution), that the Constitution was inspired, and that evil or misled people are seeking to destroy both. Parents are told to raise up their children in the ways of the Lord and to teach them to recognize and reject false teachings. It has been said that the day will soon come that no one will be able to live on borrowed light (testimony), so strong will be the buffetings of Satan. Our leaders know that those who ignore these warnings will be overcome by the "whirlwind."

Jeff Godwin, a Christian minister and researcher of the New Age Movement, states that one of the favorite New Age terms used is "Whirlwind." He then goes on to make this observation:

> What a coincidence that *MORIAH*, the all-consuming, conquering wind, is the code name used by the Grand Druid Council of 13 for their one-world antichrist plot. Witches, wizards and the Illuminati (the elite and very satanic group of global power brokers) are all waiting anxiously for this destroying New Age whirlwind to rebuild the world THEIR way.[176]

The persecutions and trials which Satan will heap upon the Saints will largely come from the peoples and organizations under the massive New Age umbrella. We are out numbered by Satan's forces, who know more and are working more diligently than we are, yet we know the Lord will prevail. The only thing which stands in doubt is who will be on the Lord's side when He comes. Will all the Saints use the light of the gospel to actively fight evil, or will many be with those who pretend that "All is well in Zion; yea, Zion prospereth, all is well—and thus the devil cheateth their souls, and leadeth them away carefully down to hell" (2 Nephi 28:21)?

What Is the Responsibility of the Saints?

President Brigham Young cautioned the early saints about their tendency to ask the Lord to solve their problems without first doing all that was within their power:

> Have I any good reason to say to my Father in Heaven, "Fight my battles," When He has given me the sword to wield, the arm and the brain that I can fight for myself? Can I ask Him to fight my battles and sit quietly down waiting for Him to do so? I cannot. I can pray the people to hearken to wisdom, to listen to counsel; but to ask God to do for me that which I can do for myself is preposterous to my mind.[177]

In order to make sure the Saints clearly understood this principle, President Ezra Taft Benson reiterated a similar statement by President Young in his Conference talk of April, 1963:

> We all believe that the Lord will fight our battles; but how? Will he do it while we are unconcerned and make no effort whatever for our own safety when the enemy is upon us? . . . it would be quite as reasonable to expect remission of sins without baptism, as to expect the Lord to fight our battles without our taking every precaution to be prepared to defend ourselves. The Lord requires us to be quite as willing to fight our own battles as to have Him fight them for us. If we are not ready for the enemy when he comes upon us, we have not lived up to the requirements of Him who guides the ship of Zion, or who dictates the affairs of His kingdom.[178]

Where would the Saints be now if they had employed this line of reasoning during the war in heaven? All who have been born on earth rejected Satan in some measure during that war. Many members of The Church of Jesus Christ of Latter-day Saints, along with countless others who know not where to find the truth, were valiant in the defense of agency and the plan of our Eternal Father as put forth by the Savior. Having acted decisively in behalf of the Lord's plan, it is expected that the same be done here, particularly of the members of the Lord's Church; for where "much is given, much is required" (D & C 82:3).

President Ezra Taft Benson tells us:

> As important as are all other principles of the gospel, it was the freedom issue which determined whether you received a body. To have been on the wrong side of the freedom issue during the war in heaven meant eternal damnation. How then can Latter-day Saints expect to be on the wrong side in this life and escape the eternal consequences? The war in heaven is raging on earth today. The issues are the same: shall men be compelled to do what others claim is for their best welfare or will they heed the counsel of the prophet and preserve their freedom?[179]

Satan hopes to entice the Saints to not get involved in this fight for the free agency of mankind. If they listen to these misleading falsehoods of Satan their eternal salvation may well be at risk.

Cheryll Lynn May explains the responsibility church members have to participate in local affairs and the possible loss of the opportunity to affect decisions if they abdicate their duty:

> ... Some members like to think that civic participation by Latter-day Saints in democratic countries is seldom appropriate. On what grounds do they arrive at such a conclusion? Some argue that since the world is presently engaged in the last tragic scenes of a drama which (as the Lord has revealed) must inevitably end in the destruction of all the kingdoms of men, it is hopeless to try to maintain (or restore) honesty, accountability, or effectiveness to one's political system. Others maintain that the demands of active Church membership leave little time or energy for engaging in "active citizenship."
>
> ... Despite these difficulties, latter-day prophets have indicated that neither the knowledge of future political collapse nor a full schedule of Church activities absolves the Latter-day Saint from the duty, at the proper time and place, of going beyond regular voting to more active levels of participation.
>
> *Political life, whether on the level of school board member, "pressure group" leader, or state governor*, refines the political skills of reasoning, persuasion, organization, and negotiation. ...

When one leaves the burden of active political participation to others, he loses the opportunity to affect directly many of the decisions that will shape his [community and] world. He abdicates a degree of control over his life and his community which he might otherwise have exercised. The Lord . . . surely cannot be pleased when those of his children blessed with a democratic form of government refuse to grasp the opportunities it offers for active civic participation and allow their potential for gaining greater understanding and mastery of self-government to atrophy. . . . Significant problems and challenges often can be met by local civic action.

. . . If men and women of character fail to participate in the political decisions that shape their lives, others with more selfish motives will inevitably rush in to fill the void.[180]

Perhaps it is forgotten that "freedom" is a major tenet of the gospel, and that the Saints are the stewards of this God-given imperative. President John Taylor has instructed that *"besides the preaching of the Gospel, we have another mission, namely, the perpetuation of the free agency of man and the maintenance of liberty, freedom, and the rights of man."*[181]

Satan will do everything he can to keep the priesthood asleep and off balance in this fight for our freedoms. President Ezra Taft Benson identified what Satan will whisper in the hearts of the Saints to lull them into inaction:

First: "We really haven't received much instruction about freedom," the devil says. *This is a lie, for we have been warned time and time again.* . . .

Second: "You're too involved in other Church work," says the devil. *But freedom is a weighty matter of the law; the lesser principles of the gospel you should keep but not leave this one undone.* . . .

Third: "You want to be loved by everyone," says the devil, "and this freedom battle is so controversial you might be accused of engaging in politics." . . .

>**Fourth:** "Wait until it becomes popular to do," says the devil, "or, at least until everybody in the church agrees on what should be done." ...
>
>**Fifth:** "It might hurt your business or your family," says the devil, "and besides why not let the gentiles save the country? They aren't as busy as you are." ...
>
>**Sixth:** "Don't worry," says the devil, "the Lord will protect you, and besides, the world is so corrupt and heading toward destruction at such a pace that you can't stop it, so why try?" *Well, to begin with, the Lord will not protect us unless we do our part.*
>
>... The Book of Mormon warns us that when we should see these murderous conspiracies in our midst that we should awake to our awful situation. Now why should we awake if the Lord is going to take care of us anyway?
>
>... For, *after all, the purpose of life is to prove ourselves and the final victory will be for freedom.*[182]

As has been shown, the New Age hopes to neutralize the Constitution in favor of a "World View." The prophets Joseph Smith and Brigham Young have said that it will be the destiny of this people to step forward and save the Constitution, the embodiment of liberty, from "threatened destruction."[183] President Ezra Taft Benson declared that the Saints have a divine calling and responsibility to preserve the Constitution:

> ... I testify that the God of Heaven sent some of His choicest spirits to lay the foundation of this government, and He has sent other choice spirits—even you who read my words—to preserve it.[184]

President Benson also said,

> For nearly six thousand years, God has held you in reserve to make your appearance in the final days before the Second Coming of the Lord. Some individuals will fall away, but the kingdom of God will remain intact to welcome the return of its Head—even Jesus Christ.

While our generation will be comparable in wickedness to the days of Noah, when the Lord cleansed the earth by flood, *there is a major difference this time: God has saved for the final inning some of His strongest and most valiant children,* who will help bear off the kingdom triumphantly. That is where you come in, for you are the generation that must be prepared to meet your God.

In all ages prophets have looked down through the corridors of time to our day. Billions of the deceased and those yet to be born have their eyes on us. Make no mistake about it—you are a marked generation. *There has never been more expected of the faithful in such a short period of time than there is of us.* Never before on the face of this earth have the forces of evil and the forces of good been so well organized. Now is the great day of the devil's power. But now is also the great day of the Lord's power, with the greatest number of priesthood holders on the earth.

Each day the forces of evil and the forces of good enlist new recruits. Each day we personally make many decisions showing the cause we support. The final outcome is certain—the forces of righteousness will finally win. But what remains to be seen is where each of us personally, now and in the future, will stand in this battle—and how tall we will stand. *Will we be true to our last days and fulfill our foreordained missions?*[185] (Emphasis added.)

What Can the Saints Do to Prepare?

If the Saints are to fulfill this momentous *foreordained mission,* they must study the Constitution and the principles set forth in it which the Lord caused to be established (D & C 101:77). They must study the scriptures, using the Holy Ghost to recognize the signs of the times, and recognize what freedoms are being threatened. The Lord knows it is crucial that these liberties *"should be maintained for the rights and protection of all flesh, . . . That every man may act . . . according to the moral agency which I have given unto him"* (D & C 101:77-78). It is impossible to remain uninformed and expect to preserve these liberties.[186]

And yet, even with this declaration of the Lord, many Saints support causes and organizations that are in direct opposition to the divinely inspired principles and freedoms set forth in the Constitution, claiming that these principles do not apply to modern problems. This type of rationalization is the deceptive whispering of Satan, who seeks "to deceive and to blind men" (Moses 4:4).

Bruce R. McConkie had this comment:

> Satan imitates the truth. God has a Church and so does the devil. There are false Christs, false prophets, false apostles, false spirits, false ministers. "In relation to the kingdom of God," the Prophet Joseph Smith said, speaking of the Church restored in this dispensation, "the devil always sets up his kingdom at the very same time in opposition to God." Also: "False prophets always arise to oppose the true prophets and they will prophesy so very near the truth that they will deceive almost the very chosen ones" (Teachings, p. 365).[187]

The First Presidency of the Church has also warned the Saints:

> Satan is making war against all the wisdom that has come to men through their ages of experience. He is seeking to overturn and destroy the very foundations upon which society, government, and religion rest. He aims to have men adopt theories and practices which he induced their forefathers, over the ages, to adopt and try, only to be discarded by them when found unsound, impractical and ruinous. He plans to destroy liberty and freedom—economic, political, and religious, and to set up in place thereof the greatest, most widespread, and most complete tyranny that has ever oppressed man.
>
> He is working under such perfect disguise that many do not recognize either him or his methods. . . . Without their knowing it, the people are being urged down paths that lead only to destruction. Satan never before had so firm a grip on this generation as he has now.[188]

President Joseph Fielding Smith taught: "There is no saying of greater truth than 'that which doth not edify is not of God.' And 'that which is not of God is darkness.' *It matters not whether it comes in the guise of religion, ethics, philosophy or revelation. No revelation from God will fail to edify."* [189] (Emphasis added.)

The dangers inherent in the New Age have all been prophesied, and current Church leaders have warned against these types of doctrines. With all that has been given it is a wonder that so many do not actively fight the freedom-killing practices of the New Age.

In 1831 the Lord gave this instruction to his church:

> For behold, it is not meet that I should command in all things; for he that is compelled in all things, the same is a slothful and not a wise servant; wherefore he receiveth no reward.
>
> Verily I say, men should be anxiously engaged in a good cause, and do many things of their own free will, and bring to pass much righteousness;
>
> For the power is in them, wherein they are agents unto themselves. And inasmuch as men do good they shall in nowise lose their reward.
>
> But he that does not anything until he is commanded, and receiveth a commandment with doubtful heart, and keepeth it with slothfulness, the same is damned (D & C 58:26-29).

Some refuse to look past the surface of events, perhaps even denying that freedom-hating, power-seeking men are operating in secret. Perhaps they have not read the Book of Mormon or listened to the brethren.

Moroni, who saw our day, warned of the wickedness and murderous combinations we would face, and he implored the Saints to respond to them:

> Wherefore, O ye Gentiles, it is wisdom in God that these things should be shown unto you, that thereby ye may repent of your sins, and suffer not that these murderous combinations shall get above you, which are built up to get power and gain— and the work, yea, even the work of destruction come upon you,

yea, even the sword of the justice of the Eternal God shall fall upon you, to your overthrow and destruction if ye shall suffer these things to be.

Wherefore, the Lord commandeth you, when ye shall see these things come among you that ye shall awake to a sense of your awful situation, because of this secret combination which shall be among you. . . .

For it cometh to pass that whoso buildeth it up seeketh to overthrow the freedom of all lands, nations, and countries; and it bringeth to pass the destruction of all people for it is built up by the devil . . . (Ether 8:23-25).

Why would the Lord have his Nephite prophets warn about the dangers of secret organizations which would deny our freedoms if there are none? Why would the lord warn that they exist unless he wanted us to know of these evils and respond decisively? The Lord expects us to be aware of and avoid Satan's snares that place the Saints in temporal and spiritual bondage.

We can use our agency to oppose Satan's work, or we can "sit upon our thrones and . . . not make use of the means which the Lord has provided for us" (Alma 60:21). Do we have the strength and courage to be alert and faithful watchmen, to make the right choices, and to take the right actions?

What Can Be Done?

As President David O. McKay has remarked: *"The fight for freedom cannot be divorced from the gospel."*[190] President McKay further stated that "references in the scriptures show that this principle [of free agency] is (1) essential to man's salvation; and (2) may become a measuring rod by which the actions of men, of organizations, of nations may be judged."[191]

President Ezra Taft Benson has warned:

"Any Christian constitutionalist who retreats from this battle jeopardizes his life here and hereafter. Seldom has so much responsibility hung on so few, so heavily; but our numbers are increasing, *and we who have been warned have a responsibility to warn our neighbor.*"[192] (Emphasis added; see also D & C 88:81.)

What then should the Saints do?

First, you must remember that "faith without works is dead" (James 2:26). You must inform yourselves and your neighbors of the deceptive teachings and false doctrines of the New Age.

Second, New Age proponents do not want Christians to become politically active. This is exactly what you must do. Become involved in your local school districts and community. Become informed of the New Age threats and let elected officials know where you stand on affected issues. Encourage them to introduce and support legislation that will defend national sovereignty, privacy and individual freedoms while opposing legislation that would threaten them.

Third, sponsor good candidates to run for office who will represent your views, or consider running for office yourself. In any circumstance, be active in the process.

Fourth, you must be aware of and review the music your family is listening to, the books they are reading, the computer games they are playing, and the movies and TV shows they are watching. Teach your children critical thinking skills so that they can analyze all the "Madison Avenue" sales hype in the advertisements. Explain how the media tries to subtly influence behavior.

Fifth, if you have fallen out of full activity in the church, come back! During these crucial latter days, you need all the Lords guidance through continuing revelation to the prophets. You must also strengthen your spirituality through prayer, asking the Lord that the truth of all things to be made known to you. Study the scriptures and words of the church leaders and fulfill your church callings with the assistance of the Holy Ghost. A balanced effort is essential to effectively combat the plans of Satan.

President Ezra Taft Benson summed up the battle in these words:

"The fight for freedom is God's fight. . . . When a man stands for freedom he stands with God. And as long as he stands for freedom he stands with God. And were he to stand alone he would still stand with God—the best company and the greatest power in or out of this world. Any man will be eternally vindicated and rewarded for his stand for freedom."[193]

May we all have the courage to live up to the expectations of the Lord, our callings, commitments and responsibilities that we agreed to in the eternities before the foundations of this world.

END NOTES

Chapter One
THE NATURE OF THE BATTLE

[1] Van Orden, Dell. "The Gospel: A Light Unto The World; A Standard To Rally Around," *Church News*, Vol. 41, No. 20, May 15, 1971, p. 3.
[2] Spencer W. Kimball, *Conference Report*, April 1971, p, 7.
[3] Dwight L. Kinman, *The World's Last Dictator*, p. 197.
[4] Henry D. Moyle, *Conference Report*, October 1947, p. 46.
[5] Marion G. Romney, *Conference Report*, October 1960, p. 75.
[6] Ezra Taft Benson, *Conference Report*, October 1963, p. 16.
[7] Bruce R. McConkie, *The Millennial Messiah*, pp. 41-42.

Chapter Two
WHAT IS THE NEW AGE MOVEMENT?

[8] See Texe Marrs, *Dark Secrets of the New Age*, pp. 11-23.
[9] See William Josiah Sutton, *The New Age Movement and The Illuminati 666,* p. 205.
[10] Gary H. Kah, *The Demonic Roots of Globalism*, pp. 28-29.
[11] Mark and Elizabeth Clare Prophet, *The Science of the Spoken Word*, p. 73.
[12] Marilyn Ferguson, *The Aquarian Conspiracy*, pp. 23-4.
[13] Peter Lalonde, *The Omega Letter*, as Quoted in *The National Educator*, October, 1988, p. 14.
[14] Orson Pratt, *Journal of Discourses*, Vol. 13, p. 70.
[15] Peter Lalonde, *One World Under Anti-Christ*, p. 16.
[16] See Gilbert Matrisciana, *Gods of the New Age*, or video of the same name.
[17] Elliot Miller, *A Crash Course on the New Age Movement*, p. 32.
[18] Constance Cumbey, *The Hidden Dangers Of The Rainbow*, pp. 54-68.
[19] Texe Marrs, *Dark Secrets of the New Age*, pp. viii-ix.
[20] See John Randolph Price, *Practical Spirituality*, p. 72.

[21] Texe Marrs, *Dark Secrets of the New Age*, p. ix.
[22] *Ibid.*, pp. 13-14.
[23] *Ibid.*, p. 191.
[24] Vera Alder, *When Humanity Comes Of Age*, p. 31.
[25] Lola Davis, *Toward a World Religion for the New Age*, p. 25.
[26] See Texe Marrs, *Dark Secrets of the New Age*, pp. 206-207.
[27] See Allan Y. Cohen, "Meher Baba and the Quest of Consciousness," in *What Is Enlightenment*, John White, editor, p. 83.
[28] See John Randolph Price, *The Superbeings*, p. 3.
[29] Texe Marrs, *Mystery Mark of the New Age*, p. 75.
[30] Constance Cumbey, *The Hidden Dangers of the Rainbow*, pp. 54-68.
[31] *Ibid,* pp. 54-68.
[32] Elliot Miller, *A Crash Course on The New Age Movement*, pp. 14-15.
[33] Stephen E. Robinson, "Warring Against The Saints Of God," *The Ensign*, January 1988, pp. 34-39.
[34] See Bruce R. McConkie, "Adversary," *Mormon Doctrine*, p 25.
[35] See Elliot Miller, *A Crash Course on the New Age Movement*, pp. 36-37.
[36] See Texe Marrs, *Dark Secrets of the New Age*, pp. 195.
[37] Peter Lalonde, *One World Under Anti-Christ*, p. 123.
[38] Gary H. Kah, *The Demonic Roots of Globalism*, pp. 161-162.
[39] Ezra Taft Benson, *Conference Report*, October 1988; *Ensign*, November 1988, p. 87.
[40] George J. Romney, compiler, *Look to God and Live*, p. 145.

Chapter Three
"THE PLAN"

[41] Texe Marrs, *Dark Secrets of the New Age*, pp. 16-17.
[42] R. Kim Davis, "I Have A Question," *Ensign*, Vol. 21, No. 3, March 1991, p. 62.
[43] Bruce R. McConkie, *Mormon Doctrine*, p. 624.

End Notes

[44] R. Kim Davis, "I Have A Question," *Ensign*, Vol. 21, No. 3, March 1991, p. 62.

[45] Constance Cumbey, *The Hidden Dangers of the Rainbow*, p. 78.

[46] Texe Marrs, *Dark Secrets of the New Age*, p. 157.

[47] See John Randolph Price, *Practical Spirituality*, pp. 18-19; as quoted by Texe Marrs in *Dark Secrets of the New Age*.

[48] See John A. Widtsoe, Editor, *Discourses of Brigham Young*, p. 111.

[49] Bruce R. McConkie, "The Coming Tests and Trials and Glory," *Ensign*, May 1980, pp. 72-73.

Chapter Four
THE EXISTENCE OF SATAN

[50] Elder James E. Faust, "The Great Imitator," *Ensign*, November 1987, p. 33.

[51] President Brigham Young, *Journal of Discourses*, Vol. 2, pp. 93-94.

[52] Also see Bruce R. McConkie, *Mormon Doctrine*, SORCERY, SPIRITUALISM, WITCHCRAFT.

[53] Bruce R. McConkie, *Doctrinal New Testament Commentary*, Vol. 3, pp. 524-525.

[54] S. H. Roundy, Unpublished Manuscript on file in the Church Historical Department in Salt Lake City, Utah.

[55] President Harold B. Lee, "A Time of Decision," *Ensign*, July 1972, pp. 29-33.

Chapter Five
WITCHCRAFT, A NEW AGE RELIGION

[56] Gary H. Kah, *The Demonic Roots of Globalism*, p. 160.

[57] *Ibid.* pp. 160-161.

[58] Gary H. Kah, *En Route to Global Occupation*, pp. 6-7.

[59] Peter Lalonde, *One World Under Anti-Christ*, p. 155.

[60] Miriam Starhawk, "Witchcraft and the Religion of the Great Goddess," *Yoga Journal*, May/June 1986, pp. 38-41.

[61] John Todd, *Salvation from Witchcraft*.

[62] *Ibid.*
[63] See William Josiah Sutton, *The New Age Movement and The Illuminati 666*, p. 173.
[64] Texe Marrs, *Dark Majesty*, p. 242.
[65] William Josiah Sutton, *The New Age Movement and The Illuminati 666*, p. 177.
[66] *Ibid.*, pp. 172-173.
[67] John Todd, *Salvation from Witchcraft*.
[68] Stan Deyo, *The Cosmic Conspiracy*, p. 70.
[69] *Ibid.*, pp. 69-79.
[70] *Ibid.*, pp. 70.
[71] John Daniel, *Scarlet and the Beast*, Vol. 1, p. 693.
[72] Stan Deyo, *The Cosmic Conspiracy*, p. 73.
[73] John Todd, *Salvation from Witchcraft*.
[74] Barry Goldwater, *With No Apologies*, p. 292.
[75] William E. Dunham, "Correction, Please!" *The Review of the News*. 9 April 1980, pp. 37-38.
[76] Gary Allen, *The Rockefeller File*, p. 77.
[77] Barry Goldwater, *With No Apologies*, pp. 4, 293, 297, 299.
[78] Christian Warner, "World Dictatorship and the New Age Movement," *Newswatch Magazine*, September 1986, p. 26.
[79] Zbigniew Brzezinski, *Between Two Ages*, as quoted by Peter Lalonde in *One World Under Anti-Christ*, p. 124.
[80] Peter Lalonde, *One World Under Anti-Christ*, p. 124.
[81] Mark Satin, *New Age Politics: Healing Self and Society*, as quoted by Peter Lalonde in *One World Under Anti-Christ*, p. 124.
[82] Liberty Lobby, *Blueprint for Dictatorship*.
[83] Mike Blair, "Your Constitutional Rights Could Disappear Overnight," FEMA vs. Your Constitutional Rights—A Special Supplement to *The Spotlight*, May 1992, p. 2.
[84] See "A Review and Commentary on Rexford G. Tugwell's book *The Emerging Constitution*" by Col. Curtis B. Dall and E. Stanley Rittenhouse.
[85] *National Spotlight*, March 29, 1976.
[86] John Taylor, *Journal of Discourses*, April 9, 1879, Vol. 21, p. 31.

[87] Erastus Snow, *Journal of Discourses*, May 31, 1885, Vol. 26, p. 226.

[88] David O. McKay, *Gospel Ideals*, p. 299.

[89] *Congressional Quarterly Special Report* supplement to Vol. 44, No. 8. February 22, 1986 pp. 458-459. Senate version S 1851 passed Feb. 19,1986. *Congressional Quarterly Weekly Report* Vol. 46, No. 43, October 22, 1988, p. 3038.

[90] See Supreme Court cases: *U.S. v. Thompson*, 258 F. 257, E.D. Ark. (1919), *U.S. v. Samples*, 258 F. 479, W.D. Mo. (1919), *Missouri v. Holland*, 252 U.S. 416, 434, 40 S. Ct. 382, 384 (1920), Also see *U.S. v. Selkirk* (1919); U.S. v. Rockefeller (1919); and *U.S. v. Lumpkin* (1921). *Cerritos Gun Club v. Hall*, 96 F. 2d 620 (9th Cir., 1938) *Bailey v. Holland*, 126 F. 2d 317 (4th Cir. 1942) *U.S. v. Jin Fuey Moy*, 241 U.S. 394, 36 S. Ct. 658 (1916) *Stutz v. Bureau of Narcotics*, 56 F. Supp. 810, 813 (N.D. Cal., 1944) *Balfour, Guthrie & Co. v. United States*, 90 F. Supp. 831 (N.D. Cal., 1950).

[91] See Peter Lalonde, *One World Under Anti-Christ*, pp. 193-194.

[92] See John Daniel, *Scarlet and the Beast*, Vol. 1, pp. 285-286.

[93] See Gilbert Matrisciana, *Gods of the New Age*, or video of the same name.

[94] Barbara Marx Hubbard, *The Apple of Eden's Eye*, 1958, as quoted by Dwight L. Kinman in *The World's Last Dictator*, p. 18b.

[95] Texe Marrs, *Mystery Mark of the New Age*, p. 153.

[96] Antero Alli, "Undoing Yourself," *Magical Blend*, Issue #16, 1987, p. 22.

[97] Djwhal Khul, channeled through Alice Bailey, "Food for Thought," *Life Times*, Winter 1986-87, p. 57.

[98] John Randolph Price, *Practical Spirituality*, p. 19.

[99] Ruth Montgomery, *Threshold to Tomorrow*, pp. 195-208.

[100] Maharishi Mahesh Yogi, *Inauguration of the Dawn of the Age of Enlightenment*, p. 47.

[101] See Christopher Hyatt as quoted in "Undoing Yourself" by Antero Alli, *Magical Blend*, Issue 16, 1987, p. 21.

[102] John-Alexis Viereck, interview with Jose Arguelles, "Earth Speaks: The Great Return, August 16-17," *Meditation,* Summer 1987, Vol. II, No. 3, pp. 6-9, 50.

[103] Tex Marrs, *Mystery Mark of the New Age,* pp. 185-186.

[104] Texe Marrs, "The Frightening Reality of New Age Occultism in Our U.S. Armed Forces," *Flashpoint,* Living Truth Ministries, September 1994, p. 3.

[105] Donald S. McAlvany, "America at the Crossroads: Freedom or Slavery?" *The McAlvany Intelligence Advisor,* August, 1994, pp. 15-16.

[106] Mortimer J. Adler, "World Peace in Truth," *Center Magazine,* March/April 1978, as quoted by Peter Lalonde, *One World Under Anti-Christ,* pp. 190-191.

[107] Robert Rosio, *Satanization of Society: Secular Humanism's Assault on America,* pp. 78-79.

Chapter Six
SATAN'S SYMBOLS AND MUSIC

[108] Constance Cumbey, *The Hidden Dangers of the Rainbow,* p. 46.

[109] See Texe Marrs, *Ravaged by the New Age,* p. 237.

[110] See William Josiah Sutton, *The New Age Movement and The Illuminati 666,* pp. 44-52.

[111] *Ibid.,* pp. 44-46, 112.

[112] *Ibid.,* p. 45.

[113] John Todd, *Salvation from Witchcraft.*

[114] Roy Allen Anderson, D.D., *The Antichrist 666,* pp. 45-46.

[115] Bruce R. McConkie, *The Mortal Messiah,* Book 1, Footnotes, p. 97.

[116] See Texe Marrs, *Mystery Mark of the New Age,* pp. 102-118. See also John Todd, *Salvation from Witchcraft.*

[117] William Josiah Sutton, *The Illuminati 666,* pp. 221-222.

[118] See Texe Marrs, *Ravaged by the New Age,* p. 208.

[119] Barbara Bernstein, "Lizards Like Symphonies but Hide from Rock," *Deseret News,* April 1981.

END NOTES

[120] Olga Curtis, "Music That Kills Plants," *Denver Post*, June 21, 1970.
[121] John K. Diamond, *Behavioral Kinesiology*, p. 100.
[122] James Girard, *American Mercury*, September, 1961, as quoted by Dorothy J. Crandall, *How Music Affects Behavior*, p. 16.
[123] Frank Zappa, "The Oracle Has It All Psyched Out," *Life*, June 28, 1968, p. 91.
[124] Rev. James J. LeBar, *Cults, Sects, and the New Age*, pp. 150-151.
[125] Ezra Taft Benson, "Satan's Thrust—Youth," *Ensign*, December 1971, pp. 53-56.
[126] Hal Williams, "Dr. Reid Nibley on Acquiring a Taste for Classical Music," *BYU Today*, April 1978, p. 15.
[127] *Rolling Stone*, May 5, 1977, p. 55.
[128] *The Playboy Interviews with John Lennon and Yoko Ono*, 1982, p. 106.
[129] Charles White, *The Life and Times of Little Richard*, pp. 206, 197.
[130] Sound track from the film *Jimi Hendrix*, Interview with Fayne Pridgon, (Side 4).
[131] *Hit Parader*, February 1978, p. 24.
[132] *Rolling Stone*, August 19, 1971, p. 49.
[133] Lex De Azevedo, *Pop Music and Morality*, p. 69.
[134] Mike Warnke with Dave Balsiger and Les Jones, *The Satan-Seller*, pp. 88, 100.
[135] See John Todd, *Salvation from Witchcraft*. Also Dorothy J. Crandall, *How Music Affects Behavior*, pp. 25-26.
[136] William Josiah Sutton, *The New Age Movement and The Illuminati 666*, pp. 125-126.
[137] Jeff Godwin, *What's Wrong with Christian Rock?*, p. 144.
[138] Randall Baer, *Inside the New Age Nightmare*, pp. 153-154.
[139] Elliot Miller, *A Crash Course on the New Age Movement*, p. 190.
[140] Texe Marrs, *Ravaged by the New Age*, p. 244.
[141] Patrick J. Harbula, "Sounds of Transformation: A Talk With Brother Charles," *Meditations*, Fall 1987, p. 20.
[142] Jeff Godwin, *What's Wrong with Christian Rock?*, p. 130.

[143] "Subliminal Tapes Big Business," *Monroe, Louisiana News-Star*, January 28, 1990.
[144] *The Love Tapes catalog*, 1988, pp. 16-17.
[145] Jeff Godwin, *What's Wrong with Christian Rock?*, p. 132.
[146] "For the Strength of Youth," pamphlet of standards endorsed by the First Presidency and Quorum of the Twelve, The Church of Jesus Christ of Latter-day Saints, pp. 13-14.
[147] *Ibid.* p. 14.

Chapter Seven
A NEW BIBLE PLANNED FOR MANKIND

[148] See Joseph Fielding Smith, compiler, *Teachings of the Prophet Joseph Smith*, p. 365.
[149] See Lola Davis, *Toward a World Religion for the New Age*, pp. 178, 180-182, 193-195, 222.
[150] Some of the Various Bible Versions Reviewed: KJV—*King James Version*, NIV—*New International Version*, NAB—*New American Bible*, ASB—*American Standard Bible*, RSV—*Revised Standard Version*.
[151] G. A. Riplinger, *New Age Bible Versions*, pp. 11-12, 15.
[152] See Madame Helena Petrovna Blavatsky, *The Secret Doctrine*, Vol. 1. pp. 73, 102, 104, 105, 125, 144, 145, 592, 614; Vol. 2. pp. 30, 247, 381, 405, 472-473, 558, 573, 580, 612, 613, 614. 617, 660.
[153] Randall N. Baer, *Inside the New Age Nightmare*, pp. 21-22.
[154] See Leon Jaroff, "A No-Touch Therapy," *Time*, November 1994, pp. 88-89.
[155] Robyn Brown, as told to Stephen R. Gorton, "A Bitter Taste of 'the Good Life,'" *Ensign*, March 1990, p. 65.
[156] Bruce R. McConkie, *Mormon Doctrine*, pp. 56, 202-203, 526, 542, 759, 840.
[157] John Todd, *Salvation from Witchcraft*.
[158] William Josiah Sutton, *The New Age Movement and the Illuminati 666*, pp. 33-34.
[159] *Ibid.*, p. 77.

[160] *Ibid.*, pp. 33-34.
[161] Randall N. Baer, *Inside the New Age Nightmare*, pp. 54-56.
[162] John A. Widtsoe, *Evidences and Reconciliations*, pp. 108-109.

Chapter Eight
WHO IS LORD MAITREYA?

[163] See Bob Larson, *Straight Answers on the New Age*, pp. 198-199. Also see Constance Cumbey, *The Hidden Dangers of the Rainbow*, pp. 19-20.
[164] See *Los Angeles Times*, Sunday, April 25, 1982, Part 1, p. 31; also see Constance Cumby, *The Hidden Dangers of the Rainbow*, Back cover.
[165] See Texe Marrs, *Dark Secrets of the New Age*, p. 59.
[166] J. Gordon Melton, *The Encyclopedia of American Religions*, pp. 60-61.
[167] Constance Cumby, *The Hidden Dangers of the Rainbow*, p. 67.
[168] See Bob Larson, *Straight Answers on the New Age*, pp. 198-199.
[169] William Norman Grigg, Senior Editor, *The New American*, Vol. 11, No. 4, February 20, 1995, pp. 16-17.
[170] Anthony J. Hilder, "Alien spooks to appear on Earth by year 2000?", *The National Educator*, October, 1992, p. 11.
[171] Texe Marrs, *Dark Majesty*, p. 95.
[172] Aric Z. Leavitt, *The Illuminati*, p. 158.
[173] Shirley Marlow, "Bush Has a Date With a Pyramid," *Los Angeles Times*, January 3, 1989, p. 10. Also see "Millennium Group Expects Bush at '99 Egypt Bash," *The Arizona Daily Star*, January 3, 1989, Section A, p. 5.
[174] See John Randolph Price, *Practical Spirituality*, p. 72.

Chapter Nine
WHAT IS THE RESPONSIBILITY OF THE SAINTS?

[175] Elder Dallin H. Oaks, of the Quorum of the Twelve Apostles, *Ensign*. October 1994, pp. 13-14.
[176] Jeff Godwin, *What's Wrong with Christian Rock*, pp. 145-146.

[177] Brigham Young, *Journal of Discourses*, Vol. 12, p. 241.
[178] Brigham Young, *Journal of Discourses*, Vol. 11, p. 131, as quoted by Ezra Taft Benson, *Conference Report*, April 1963, p. 113.
[179] Ezra Taft Benson, *An Enemy Hath Done This*, p. 274.
[180] Cheryll Lynn May, "Beyond Voting," *Ensign*, June, 1976, pp. 46-48.
[181] John Taylor, *Journal of Discourses*, Vol. 23, p. 63.
[182] Ezra Taft Benson, *An Enemy Hath Done This*, pp. 275-278.
[183] See Brigham Young, *Journal of Discourses*, Vol. 2, p. 182, & Vol. 7, p. 15.
[184] *The Teachings of Ezra Taft Benson*, p. 614.
[185] Ezra Taft Benson, *In His Steps,* Dedication of Boise Institute of Religion Building.
[186] See *The Teachings of Ezra Taft Benson*, p. 619.
[187] Bruce R McConkie, *Doctrinal New Testament Commentary*, Vol. 2, p. 440.
[188] "Messages of the First Presidency," *Conference Report*, October 1942, p. 13.
[189] Joseph Fielding Smith, *Church History and Modern Revelation*, Vol. 1, pp. 201-202.
[190] Ezra Taft Benson, *An Enemy Hath Done This*, p. 306.
[191] David O. McKay, *Gospel Ideals*, pp. 299-300.
[192] *The Teachings of Ezra Taft Benson*, p. 591.
[193] Ezra Taft Benson, *An Enemy Hath Done This*, pp. 54-55.

BIBLIOGRAPHY

Adler, Mortimer J. "World Peace in Truth," *Center Magazine.* March/April 1978.
Alder, Vera. *When Humanity Comes of Age.* Austin, Texas: Quartus Books. 1985.
Allen, Gary. *The Rockefeller File.* Seal Beach, California: '76 Press, 1976.
Alli, Antero. "Undoing Yourself," *Magical Blend*, Issue 16. 1987.
Anderson, Roy Allan, D.D., editor. *The Antichrist 666.* U.S.A.: Workers for God, Inc. 1980.
Baer, Randall. *Inside the New Age Nightmare.* Lafeyette, Louisiana: Huntington House, Inc. 1989.
Benson, Ezra Taft. *An Enemy Hath Done This.* Salt Lake City, Utah: Parliament Publishers. 1969.
Benson, Ezra Taft. *Conference Report.* Salt Lake City, Utah: Corporation of the President of The Church of Jesus Christ of Latter-day Saints. April, 1963.
Benson, Ezra Taft. *Conference Report.* Salt Lake City, Utah: Corporation of the President of The Church of Jesus Christ of Latter-day Saints. October, 1963.
Benson, President Ezra Taft. Dedication of the Boise, Idaho Institute of Religion Building.
Benson, President Ezra Taft. "I Testify," *Ensign*, Volume 18, Number 11. Salt Lake City, Utah: Corporation of the President of The Church of Jesus Christ of Latter-day Saints. November, 1988.
Benson, Elder Ezra Taft. "Satan's Thrust—Youth," *Ensign*, Salt Lake City, Utah: Corporation of the President of The Church of Jesus Christ of Latter-day Saints. December, 1971.
Benson, President Ezra Taft. *Teachings of Ezra Taft Benson.* Salt Lake City, Utah: Bookcraft. 1988.

Bernstein, Barbara. "Lizards Like Symphonies but Hide from Rock," *Deseret News*. Salt Lake City, Utah: Deseret News Press. April 1981.

Blair, Mike. "Your Constitutional Rights Could Disappear Overnight," FEMA vs Your Constitutional Rights—Special Supplement to The SPOTLIGHT. Washington, D.C.: The Spotlight. May, 1992.

Blavatsky, Madame Helena Petrovna. *The Secret Doctrine*, Volume One.

Blueprint For Dictatorship. Washington, D.C.: Liberty Lobby. 1972.

Brown, Robyn, as told to Stephen R. Gorton. "A Bitter Taste of 'the Good Life'," *Ensign*, Volume 20, Number 3. Salt Lake City, Utah: Corporation of the President of The Church of Jesus Christ of Latter-day Saints. March, 1990.

Brzezinski, Zbigniew. *Between Two Ages*. New York, New York: Viking Press. 1970.

Cohen, Allan Y. "Meher Baba and the Quest of Consciousness," in *What Is Enlightenment*, John White, Editor.

Congressional Quarterly, Washington D.C., Government Printing House.

Crandall, Dorothy J. *How Music Affects Behavior*. Doctoral Dissertation. Brigham Young University. April 1984.

Cumbey, Constance. *The Hidden Dangers of the Rainbow*. Shreveport, Louisiana: Huntington House, Inc. 1983.

Curtis, Olga. "Music That Kills Plants," *Denver Post*. Denver, Colorado. June 21, 1970.

Dall, Col. Curtis B. and Rittenhouse, E. Stanley. "A Review and Commentary on Rexford G. Tugwell's Book 'The Emerging Constitution'." Washington, D.C.: Liberty Lobby. April, 1976.

Daniel, John. *Scarlet and the Beast, A History of the War between English and French Freemasonry*, Volume 1. Tyler, Texas: Jon Kregel, Inc. 1994.

Davis, Lola. *Toward a World Religion for the New Age*.

Davis, R. Kim. "I Have A Question," *Ensign*, Volume 21, No. 3. Salt Lake City, Utah: Corporation of the President of The Church of Jesus Christ of Latter-day Saints. March, 1991.

De Azevedo, Lex. *Pop Music and Morality*. Embryo Books. 1982.

Deyo, Stan. *The Cosmic Conspiracy*. Kalamunda, Western Australia: West Australian Texas Trading. 1978.

Diamond, John K. *Behavioral Kinesiology*. Harper and Row. 1982.

Dunham, William E. "Correction, Please!" *The Review of the News*. 9 April 1980.

Faust, Elder James E. "The Great Imitator," *Ensign*, Salt Lake City, Utah: Corporation of the President of The Church of Jesus Christ of Latter-day Saints. November, 1987.

Ferguson, Marilyn. *The Aquarian Conspiracy*. Los Angeles, California: J. P. Tarcher, Inc. 1980.

"For the Strength of Youth." Salt Lake City, Utah: The Corporation of the President of The Church of Jesus Christ of Latter-day Saints. 1990.

Girard, James. *American Mercury*. September 1961.

Gods of the New Age, a video. Jeremiah Films, Inc. 1988.

Godwin, Jeff. *What's Wrong with Christian Rock?* Chino, California: Chick Publications. 1990.

Goldwater, Barry M. *With No Apologies*. New York, New York: Berkley Books. 1980.

Harbula, Patrick J. "Sounds of Transformation: A Talk With Brother Charles," *Meditations*. Fall 1987.

Hilder, Anthony J. "Alien spooks to appear on Earth by year 2000?" *The National Educator*. Fullerton, California. October, 1992.

Hit Parader. February 1978.

Hubbard, Barbara Marx. *The Apple of Eden's Eye*. 1958.

Hyatt, Christopher, as quoted by Antero Alli. "Undoing Yourself," *Magical Blend*. 1987.

Jaroff, Leon. "A No-Touch Therapy," *Time*, Volume 144. New York, New York: Time Incorporated. November 21, 1994.

"Jimi Hendrix." Soundtrack from the film. Interview with Fayne Pridgon. Side 4.

Kah, Gary H. *The Demonic Roots of Globalism.* Lafayette, Louisiana: Huntington House Publishers. 1995.

Kah, Gary H. *En Route to Global Occupation.*

Khul, Djwhal, channeled through Alice Bailey. "Food for Thought," *Life Times*, Winter 1986-1987.

Kimball, Spencer W. *Conference Reports.* Salt Lake City, Utah: Corporation of the President of The Church of Jesus Christ of Latter-day Saints. April, 1971.

Kinman, Dwight L. *The World's Last Dictator.* Woodburn, Oregon. Solid Rock Books, Inc. Second Edition, 1995.

Lalonde, Peter, Editor. *The Omega Letter*, as Quoted in *The National Educator*. October, 1988.

Lalonde, Peter. *One World Under Anti-Christ.* Eugene, Oregon: Harvest House Publishers. 1991.

Larson, Bob. *Straight Answers on the New Age.* Nashville, Tennessee: Thomas Nelson, Inc. 1989.

Leavitt, Aric Z. *The Illuminati.* Los Angeles, California: Daystar Publications. 1994.

LeBar, Rev. James J. *Cults, Sects, and the New Age.* Huntington, Indiana: Our Sunday Visitor Publishing Division. 1989.

Lee, President Harold B. "A Time of Decision," *Ensign*. Salt Lake City, Utah: Corporation of the President of The Church of Jesus Christ of Latter-day Saints. July, 1972.

Love Tapes, catalog. Edina, Minnesota. 1988.

Marlow, Shirley. "Bush Has a Date with a Pyramid," *Los Angeles Times*. January 3, 1989.

Marrs, Texe. *Dark Majesty.* Austin, Texas: Living Truth Publishers. 1992.

Marrs, Texe. *Dark Secrets of the New Age.* Westchester, Illinois: Crossway Books. 1987.

Marrs, Texe. "The Frightening Reality of New Age Occultism in Our U.S. Armed Forces," *Flashpoint*. Austin, Texas: Living Truth Ministries. September, 1994.

Marrs, Texe. *Mystery Mark of the New Age.* Westchester, Illinois: Crossway Books. 1988.

Marrs, Texe. *Ravaged by the New Age*. Austin, Texas: Living Truth Publishers. 1989.

Matrisciana, Gilbert. *Gods of the New Age*. Eugene, Oregon: Harvest House Publishers. 1985.

May, Cheryll Lynn. "Beyond Voting," *Ensign*, Salt Lake City, Utah: Corporation of the President of The Church of Jesus Christ of Latter-day Saints. June, 1976.

McAlvany, Donald S., *The McAlvany Intelligence Advisor*. Phoenix, Arizona: The McAlvany Intelligence Advisor. August, 1994.

McConkie, Bruce R. *Doctrinal New Testament Commentary*, Volume One. Salt Lake City, Utah: Bookcraft. 1973.

McConkie, Bruce R. *Doctrinal New Testament Commentary*, Volume Two. Salt Lake City, Utah: Bookcraft. 1973.

McConkie, Bruce R. *Doctrinal New Testament Commentary*, Volume Three. Salt Lake City, Utah: Bookcraft. 1973.

McConkie, Bruce R. "The Coming Tests and Trials and Glory," *Ensign*. Salt Lake City, Utah: Corporation of the President of The Church of Jesus Christ of Latter-day Saints. May, 1980.

McConkie, Bruce R. *The Millennial Messiah*. Salt Lake City, Utah: Deseret Book Company. 1982.

McConkie, Bruce R. *Mormon Doctrine*. Salt Lake City, Utah: Bookcraft. 1966.

McConkie, Bruce R. *The Mortal Messiah*. Salt Lake City, Utah: Deseret Book Company. 1979.

McKay, David O. *Gospel Ideals*. Salt Lake City, Utah: Deseret News Press. 1953.

Melton, J. Gordon. *The Encyclopedia of American Religions*. Detroit, Michigan: Gale Research Company. 1987.

Messages of the First Presidency. *Conference Report*. Salt Lake City, Utah: Corporation of the President of The Church of Jesus Christ of Latter-day Saints. October, 1942.

Miller, Elliot. *A Crash Course on The New Age Movement*. Grand Rapids Michigan: Baker Book House. October 1990.

Montgomery, Ruth. *Threshold to Tomorrow*. New York, New York: Fawcett Press. 1982.

Moyle, Henry D. *Conference Report*. Salt Lake City, Utah: Corporation of the President of The Church of Jesus Christ of Latter-day Saints. October 1947.

National Spotlight. Washington, D. C.: Liberty Lobby. March 29, 1976.

Oaks, Elder Dallin H. "Our Strength Can Become Our Downfall," *Ensign*, Volume 24 Number 10. Salt Lake City, Utah: Corporation of the President of The Church of Jesus Christ of Latter-day Saints. October 1994.

"Playboy Interviews with John Lennon and Yoko Ono, The." Berkley, California. 1982.

Pratt, Orson. *Journal of Discourses*, Volume 13. Salt Lake City, Utah. 1967. Photo Lithographic Reprint of Exact Original Edition. Liverpool, England. 1871.

Price, John Randolph. *Practical Spirituality*. Austin, Texas: Quartus Books. 1985.

Price, John Randolph. *The Superbeings*. Austin, Texas: Quartus Books. 1981.

Riplinger, G. A. *New Age Bible Versions*. Munroe Falls, Ohio: A. V. Publications. 1993.

Robinson, Stephen E. "Warring Against The Saints of God," *Ensign*. Salt Lake City, Utah: Corporation of the President of The Church of Jesus Christ of Latter-day Saints. January, 1988.

Rolling Stone. August 19, 1971.

Rolling Stone. May 5, 1977.

Romney, George J., compiler. *Look to God and Live, Discourses of Marion G. Romney*. Salt Lake City, Utah: Deseret Book Company. 1971.

Romney, Marion G. *Conference Report*. Salt Lake City, Utah: Corporation of The President of the Church of Jesus Christ of Latter-day Saints. October, 1960.

Rosio, Robert. *Satanization of Society: Secular Humanism's Assault on America*. Lafayette, Louisiana: Prescott Press, Inc. 1994.

Roundy, S. H. "Conversation with Lucifer, His Satanic Majesty." Unpublished manuscript on file in the LDS Church Historian's Office, Salt Lake City, Utah.

Satin, Mark. *New Age Politics: Healing Self and Society*. New York, New York: Dell Publishing Co. 1978.

Smith, Joseph Fielding. *Church History and Modern Revelation*, Volume One. Salt Lake City, Utah: Deseret Book Company. 1953.

Smith, Joseph Fielding, compiler. *Teachings of the Prophet Joseph Smith*. Salt Lake City, Utah: Deseret Book Company. 1976.

Snow, Erastus. *Journal of Discourses*, Volume 26. Salt Lake City, Utah. 1967. Photo Lithographic Reprint of Exact Original Edition. Liverpool, England. 1886.

Starhawk, Miriam. "Witchcraft and the Religion of the Great Goddess," *Yoga Journal*. Berkley, California: May/June 1986.

"Subliminal Tapes Big Business," *Monroe, Louisiana News-Star*. January 28, 1990.

Sutton, William Josiah, compiler. *The New Age Movement and The Illuminati 666*. USA: The Institute of Religious Knowledge. 1983.

Taylor, John. *Journal of Discourses*, Volume 21. Salt Lake City, Utah. 1967. Photo Lithographic Reprint of Exact Original Edition. Liverpool, England. 1881.

Taylor, John. *Journal of Discourses*, Volume 23. Salt Lake City, Utah. 1967. Photo Lithographic Reprint of Exact Original Edition. Liverpool, England. 1883.

Todd, John. *Salvation From Witchcraft*. An audio cassette tape of a talk given in the mid 1970's which is in the possession of David N. Balmforth.

Van Orden, Dell. "The Gospel: A Light Unto The World; A Standard To Rally Around," *Church News* (California Edition). Volume 41, No. 20. Salt Lake City, Utah: Deseret News Publishing Co. January 14, 1971.

Viereck, John-Alexis. "Earth Speaks: The Great Return," Interview with Jose Arguelles, *Meditation*, Volume II, No. 3. August 16-17, Summer 1987.

Warner, Christian. "World Dictatorship and the New Age Movement," Newswatch Magazine. September 1986.

Warnke, Mike with Dave Balsiger and Les Jones. *The Satan Seller*. South Plainfield, New Jersey: Bridge Publishing, Inc. 1972.

White, Charles. *The Life and Times of Little Richard*. New York, New York: Harmony Books. 1984.

Widtsoe, John A., editor. *Discourses of Brigham Young*. Salt Lake City, Utah: Deseret Book Company. 1961.

Widtsoe, John A. *Evidences and Reconciliations*. Salt Lake City, Utah: Bookcraft. 1960.

Williams, Hal. "Dr. Reid Nibley on Acquiring a Taste for Classical Music," *BYU Today*. Provo, Utah: Brigham Young University. April 1978.

Yogi, Maharishi Mahesh. *Inauguration of the Dawn of the Age of Enlightenment*. Fairfield, Iowa: Maharishi International University Press. 1975.

Young, Brigham. *Journal of Discourses*, Volume 2. Salt Lake City, Utah. 1967. Photo Lithographic Reprint of Exact Original Edition. Liverpool, England. 1855.

Young, Brigham. *Journal of Discourses*, Volume 11. Salt Lake City, Utah. 1967. Photo Lithographic Reprint of Exact Original Edition. Liverpool, England. 1868.

Young, Brigham. *Journal of Discourses*, Volume 12. Salt Lake City, Utah. 1967. Photo Lithographic Reprint of Exact Original Edition. Liverpool, England. 1869.

Zapa, Frank. "The Oracle Has It All Psyched Out," *Life Magazine*. June 28, 1968.

INDEX

—A—

Adler, Mortimer J., 79
Age of Aquarius: 124, Space probe to ignite, 125
Age of Enlightenment: Those not attuned to will not survive, 52
Alder, Vera, 33
All Seeing Eye, 65
Allen, Gary, 142
Alli, Antero, 143
Altered States Of Consciousness: New Agers heavily extol, 37
Ancient prophets: Warn us to protect our freedoms, 16
Anderson, Roy Allan, 85
Animal-Magnetism, 29
Ankh: A cross with loop on top, 87; Means you despise virginity, 87
Anti-Christ. See Lord Maitreya; A powerful leader will come before the Savior returns, 123; An occult army of millions predisposed to accept him, 120; He will curse God, 123; Is he Lord Maitreya, 117; Is he possessed, 117; Make war and overcome the saints, 123; New Agers will be betrayed by him, 123; Spirit guides to help pave way, 47; Spiritualism will make his appearance possible, 114; To unite and lead World Religion and oversee One World Order, 47
Anti-proselyting law, 73
Apostasy: To precede Second Coming, 14
Arguelles, Jose, 75
Astrology. See Witchcraft; Claims to interpret the will of the star Gods, 112; Cornerstone of witchcraft, 112; Gods of, were gods of Pagans, 113, Lucifer the author of, 113
Atlantis: Lost occult knowledge being rediscovered now, 13; Occult civilization destroyed, 13; Occult pre-flood society, 13

—B—

Bach: Said music should be nothing but glory of god, 93
Backward Masking: Found in Beatles and other rock groups, 96
Baer, Randall N., 97, 108, 114
Bailey, Alice, 24, 26, 33, 74, 122; Died in 1949, 24
Barol, Bill, 99
Beatles, 94; Evil messages found in their music, 96
Beethoven: Music inspired by the Holy Spirit, 94
Benson, Ezra Taft, 19, 43, 92, 129, 130, 131, 132, 136, 137, 148
Bernstein, Barbara, 144
Bible comparisons of scriptures, 105-107
Bibliography, 149
Bill of Rights: Superseded by treaty law, 72
Blair, Mike, 142
Blavatsky, Madame Helena Petrovna, 23, 107, 146; Outlined "The Plan," 24
Book Of Mormon: Warns to awake to conspiracies, 132
Brahms: Said an atheist could not be a great composer, 94
Brown, Robyn, 109-111
Brzezinski, Zbigniew, 68; Co-created Trilateral Commission, 67

—C—

Cayce, Edgar: Said Christ already reincarnated several, 33
Channeled Entities. See Evil spirits; Teach about a cosmic Christ, 33
Channon, Lieutenant Colonel Jim, 76
Chapman, Mark David, 97
Church of the Devil: 18; "Contend against no church" except the, 17; Whoso belongeth not to Lamb's Church belongs to, 19
Church of the Lamb of God: All to belong to conspiratorial church except, 16
Churches: Only two, the Lamb's and the Devil's, 19
Clarke, Arthur C., 125
Classical Music: People became calm and peaceful, 91
Cleansing: To wipe Christians from the earth, 52

Cleveland, Harland: Originated concept of Piecemeal Functionalism, 68
Clinton Administration: Proposed anti-Christian regulations, 77
Cohen, Allan Y., 140
Conferences: Lucifer holds own, 57
Conjure Demons: How to in writings of Solomon, 85
Conspiracy: New Age calls it "The Plan," 24
Constitution: Lord "suffered to be established," 133; Saved by the Elders of Israel, 132
Conversation with Lucifer, His Satanic Majesty, 56
Cooper, J. Finley, 33
Cosmic Christ. See *False Christs*
Council on Foreign Relations, 66
Crandall, Dorothy J., 144, 145
Creme, Benjamin, 117, 120, 121; Placed ads in announcing Lord Maitreya, 117
Crest of Solomon: Also called hexagram for thousands of years, 85
Criss, Peter, 95
Cross/Ankh: Combination of two ancient symbols, 87
Cumbey, Constance, 30, 37, 83, 147
Curtis, Olga, 144

—D—

Dall, Col. Curtis B., 142
Daniel, John, 73, 142, 143
Dark Ages: Babylonian mystery teachings prevailed, 75; Knowledge restricted to elite few, 103
Davis, Lola, 33, 146
Davis, R. Kim, 48
De Azevedo, Lex, 95
Dedication, 5
Demonic Entities: Invited to posses human bodies, 35
Demonic Instructions: Take directives public in 1975, 83
Demons: Direct New Age warriors, 75; Filled with hatred, 115; Imitate God, 63

Devilism: Manifested under scientific, 29
Deyo, Stan, 65
Diamond, John K., 90
Dollar bill: On the back is seal of Illuminati, 65
Dunham, William E.,

—E—

Eastern Meditation. See Possession; An emptying of the mind, 75; Emptying oneself out a spiritual laxative, 75
Eastern Star Symbol: Two points up five-pointed star, 84
Elena: A Devil promoting New Age doctrine, 35; John Randolph Price's spiritual messenger, 35
End Notes, 139
Evil Spirits: Contact through altered state of consciousness, 35; Deny existence of God and the Son, 34; Many people today communicating with, 34
Executive orders: Laws made by one man, 69
Externalization of the Hierarchy: Alice Bailey's book on how to destroy Christianity, 24

—F—

Fahey, John, 98
False Christs. See Master Messiahs; A great world savior to appear, 43; Priesthood power needed to detect, 43; Will show great signs and wonders, 44
False Spirits: Predominant in world today, 60
Faust, James E., 55
Ferguson, Marilyn: Outlines infiltration of schools, 38
First Earth Battalion: New Age warrior-soldiers, 76
First Presidency Statement: Satan plans the most widespread and complete tyranny ever, 101, 134
Foreword, 9
Free Agency: Avoid that would deprive us of, 17; Divided over before we came here, 19; Necessary for our eternal salvation, 17; Perpetuation of also mission of Saints, 131; Should not command in all things, 135

Freedom: Issue that determined whether you received a body, 130
Freedom of choice: More treasured than any possession earth can give, 71
French Revolution: Planned by Adam Weishaupt, 64

—G—

Galileo Space Probe: To ignite in Jupiter's atmosphere, 125
Gardner, Richard, 68
Genocide Act: A treaty that supersedes the Constitution, 72; Can put you in federal prison for converting someone from another faith, 72; Signed into law in 1988, 72
Girard, James, 90
Goat head: Representative of devil, 84
Godwin, Jeff, 97, 99, 128
Goldwater, Senator Barry, 67
Gorton, Stephen R., 146
Gospel: Freedom, most important principle of, 130; New Age movement opposed to, 51; Perpetuation of free agency another mission of Saints, 131; Teaches of literal spirit children, 49; Teaches prayer to personal God, 50; Teaches we can return to Father through atonement of Jesus, 49
Graham, Billy, 81
Great and Abominable Church: Devil is the founder, 18; Had dominion over all the earth, 19; Means immense assembly or association, 40
Grigg, William Norman, 147

—H—

Halpern, Steven, 98
Harbula, Patrick J., 145
Heavenly Father: New Age beliefs lead away from, 49
Heline, Corinne, 52
Hendrix, Jimi, 94
Hexagram: Also called Crest of Solomon, 85; Means to hex or practice black magic, 85
Hilder, Anthony, 147

Hinduism: Believes in many reincarnations, 49
Holistic Health: Discernment of Holy Ghost needed, 108; Many disillusioned with the medical establishment, 108; New Age has moved aggressively into, 108; Occult laying on of hands, 109; Pushes healing by crystals and yoga, 109
Horn, Paul, 98
House of Rothschild, 65
Hubbard, Barbara Marx, 74
Human Sacrifice: In writings of Solomon, 85
Hyatt, Christopher, 74, 75

—I—

Illuminati: A Luciferian movement, 65; Destroy Christianity with humanism, 64; Founded May 1, 1776 by Adam Weishaupt, 65; Is Council on Foreign Relations in America, 66; Members of CFR are initiated into, 66; Religion is witchcraft, 64; Satanic jewelry attracts demons, 83; Their seal on back of dollar bill, 65; Witchcraft religion of, 64
Index, 157
Italian Horn: Also known as the Unicorn's Horn, 88

—J—

Jaroff, Leon, 146
Jesus Christ: Edgar Cayce said he had already reincarnated, 33; Iniquity shall abound in the day, 13; New Age believes sacrifice on cross meaningless, 32; Spirit entities antagonistic towards, 40
John, Elton, 96
Jurriaase, Aart, 122

—K—

Kah, Gary H., 24, 42, 61
Kuhl, Djwhal: Alice Bailey's Spirit Guide (Demon), 24, 74; Also known as the Tibetan, 26
Kimball, Spencer W., 13
Kinman, Dwight L., 13, 143

Kissinger, Henry, 24
Knight, J.Z.: Channel for Rathma, 26

—L—

Lalonde, Peter, 27, 41, 62, 68, 142, 143, 144
Larson, Bob, 91, 147
Last Days: New diseases and plagues will assail mankind, 12
Latter-day Saints: May be opposed by both other Christians and New Age, 52; Some depict Church as a cult, 51; Those of "the covenant," 44
Leach, Monte, 121
Leavitt, Aric Z., 125
LeBar, Rev. James J., 91
Lee, Harold B., 60
Lennon, John, 97
Liberties: Should be maintained for all flesh, 133
Little Richard, 94
Lord Maitreya. See Anti Christ; Christians view him as an anti-Christ, 121; Is he possessed, 117; Is he the anti-Christ, 117; Living in London since 1977, 117; Newspaper ad announcing, 117; Says all mankind will be introduced to ancient mysteries, 121; Says Jesus lives in Rome, 121; Says Jesus was only a temporary Christ, 121; Will reveal himself when mankind is ready, 120
Lucifer: Admits 6000 years his allotted time, 59; Also known as the "One," 107; Author of Astrology, 113; Author of spiritualism, 58; Claims Jesus stole his crown, 56; God of witches, 64; Great Imitator, 56; Has own priesthood, 57; His agents report to him, 58; His servants answer spiritualists, 58; Name removed from some new bible versions, 105; Retained pre-mortal knowledge, 57; Ruler of one world government, 65; Seeks misery of mankind, 59; Tried to destroy Joseph Smith, 58; Will impersonate Jesus Christ before real Second Coming, 113
Lucis Trust, 24, 42; Formerly Lucifer Publishing founded by Alice Bailey, 24

—M—

Marlow, Shirley, 147
Marrs, Texe, 31, 32, 36, 47, 52, 64, 74, 75, 76, 99, 125, 139, 140, 143, 144, 147
Master Messiahs. See False Christs; To appear to all major religions, 38
Matrisciana, Gilbert, 139, 143
May, Cheryll Lynn, 130
McAlvany, Donald S., 77
McConkie, Bruce R., 20, 50, 53, 56, 86, 134, 141; Various occult definitions, 111-112
McKay, David O., 71, 136
McNamara, Robert, 24
Melton, Dr. J. Gordon, 120
Miller, Elliot, 30, 38, 98, 140
Mind Sciences: Part of New Age Movement, 34
Montgomery, Ruth, 36, 75
Moral Agency: Lord gives all men, 133
Moroni: Warns of latter-day murderous combinations, 135
Mother of Abominations: Did fight against the Lamb of God, 19
Moyle, Henry D., 17
Mystical Experiences: Glue binding New Age devotees, 30

—N—

National Emergency. See Executive Orders; The President would use Executive Orders to call a, 69
Nellis Atomic Test Site (area 51), 125
Nephite Prophets: Warn our day of secret organizations, 136
New Age Battalion, 76
New Age Bible: Compared with King James Version, 105-107; Contain the benefits of occultism, 34; Lucifer's name completely removed, 105; New discoveries to change scripture, 104
New Age Leaders: Believe Jesus neither God nor Christ, 48; To outlaw some religious practices, 38; World crises and purification coming for unbelievers, 52

New Age Movement: A narcissistic religion, 32; Avowed aim to become only world religion, 31; Believe "the Christ" is an office gained through many reincarnations, 107; Believe demons are teachers, therefore good, 35; Bound by interest in the occult, 32; Communicates by supernatural chanting, drugs, spirit guides etc., 50; Denies a personal God, 49; Denies need for a Savior, 49; Embraces occult beliefs, 23; Go public with directives in 1975, 83; Has master plan to overthrow Christianity, 24; Has moved into Holistic Health, 108; Hatred for Jews and Christians, 38; Heart of is rejection of hope in Jesus Christ, 29; Includes thousands of supporting organizations, 31; Individuals and organizations bound together by common values and vision, 39; Jesus Christ sacrifice futile, 32; Main objectives: A New World Order and A New World Religion, 36; Mystical experiences glue binding, 30; Penetrated private, religious and professional areas of our lives, 36; Practice occult meditation, 75; Satan's teachings brought Dark Ages, 103; Spiritual adhesive for One Worldism, 29; Taken on the form of a religion, 31; Teaches a world teacher will lead us into a "One World Order," 123; Teaches God is; Ultimate reality or life-force, 49; Teachings pushed around the globe, 48; To cleanse Christians from earth, 52; To create New scriptures, 104

New Age Music: Can be more deadly to spirit than heavy metal rock, 99; Creates trance like state, 99; Great for visualizations, 98

New Age World Religion: A main goal of the New Age Movement, 36; And science will become one, 48; Excludes only those who believe in Jesus Christ, 31; Idolatrous religion of ancient Babylon, 47; Man neither sinful or evil, 32; Master Messiahs to persuade of truths in, 38; Mirror ancient Babylonian society, 25; Rallying cry will be World Peace, Love and Unity, 48; Satan's teachings brought Dark Ages, 103; Those who refuse to affiliate are inferior, 52; Will have a Luciferic initiation, 52; Will have New Revelation, 38

New Christ: Those who cannot accept sent to another dimension, 52

New One World Order: Goal of the New Age Movement, 36; Illuminati and world leaders calling for, 124; New Age Movement spiritual adhesive for, 29

New World Religion: New set of scriptures to cement together, 32

Nibley, Dr. Reid, 93

Nibley, Richard, 92

Noah: Evil now as bad as days of, 12

—O—

Oaks, Dallin H., 127

One World Government: Its leader will be Lucifer, 65

Ono, Yoko. See Beatles; 94, 97.

Osburn, Ozzy, 95

—P—

Pagan Superstitions: Counterfeits of true gifts, 55

Peace Symbol: Inverted broken cross, 36; Means rejection of Christianity to a witch, 87

Pentagram. See Witchcraft; Five pointed star, 84; Two points upward, 84

Piecemeal Functionalism, 68

Possession: An emptying of the mind, 75

Practical Spirituality: Outlines eradication of two billion people, 53

Pratt, Orson, 28

Price, John Randolph, 35, 53, 139, 147; Spirit guide told him one-half billion might perish in coming chaos, 74

Pridgon, Fayne, 94

Priesthood: And Spirit of Christ ample shield against Satan, 45; Holy Ghost detects false Christs, 43; Lucifer has his own, 57; Lucifer only obeys when exercised in faith, 57; Lucifer tries to offset their power, 58; Those valiant in defense of free agency, 129

Prophet, Elizabeth Clare, 27, 33

Pyramid: Capstone with eye is the Rothschild family or ruling tribunal of Illuminati, 65

—R—

Raine, George, 99
Ramtha, 26
Read, Anne, 33
Reagan, Ronald: Signed Genocide Act, 72
Regan, Donald, 24
Reincarnation: Hinduism also believes in many existence's through, 49; Or the transmigration of souls a false doctrine, 50
Retallack, Dorothy: Study of classical music, 89
Richards, Keith, 94
Riplinger, G. A., 104
Rittenhouse, E. Stanley, 142
Roberts, Jan, 26
Robinson, Stephen E., 39
Rock Music: It stirs up a warlike nature, 101; Satan is its source of inspiration, 94; Stirs rebellion, 101
Rockefeller, David, 24; Co-created Trilateral Commission, 67
Rolling Stones, 94
Romney, George J., 140
Romney, Marion G., 18, 45
Rosio, Pastor Robert, 80
Roundy, Samuel H., 56, 59
Ryerson, Kevin, 33

—S—

Saints: Anti-Christ will overcome, 123; Conspiratorial Organization to make war against, 16; Deception will not make us exempt from the justice of God, 116; Duty to have a knowledge of evil and its consequences, 55; Excuses about getting involved, 131; Many believe evil spirit entities do not exist, 34; May become caught between New Age and Christians, 52; No excuses for not doing civic duty, 130; Satan marshaling his forces to war against, 53
Satan: Caused man to commit murder, 14; Deceives by counterfeiting truth, 114; Father of all lies, 14; Great power to tempt and darken minds, 59; Imitates truth, 134; Knows time is

short, 114; Many to believe his lying spirits, 34; Marshaling forces against Saints, 53; Mastermind behind social problems, 14; Name means enemy of righteousness, 40; Planning widespread tyranny, 134; Thirteen-point master plan, 47; To conquer we must recognize, 45; Tried to destroy man's agency, 60; Wants to keep priesthood asleep, 131

Satin, Mark, 69

Schultz, George, 24

Seance: Called trance-channeling session, 28

Second Coming: A powerful leader will come before the, 123; Apostasy to precede, 14; Do not bury heads or panic as it approaches, 45

Self Improvement Seminars: Even Satan and his followers would gain celestial kingdom, 110; Ideal New Age vehicles, 109; No need to strive for perfection, 110; Promise to help achieve all your goals in life, 110; Some concepts contrary to teachings of Jesus Christ, 110; Some have the effect of brainwashing, 110

Smith, Joseph, 70, 132, 134; Lucifer tried to destroy, 58

Smith, Joseph Fielding, 146; 1971 speech at Ricks College, 12-13

Snow, Erastus, 71

Sodom and Gomorrah, 81

Solomon: Embraced false gods, 87; First to allow sacrifice of children, 86; Greatest male witch, 85; Lost his wisdom, 87; Wives turned his heart, 85; Wrote Witchcraft Bible, 85

Spangler, David, 38, 52

Spirit Guides: Antagonistic toward Jesus Christ, 40; Help man inaugurate New Age, 47; Imitate God, 63; Link up with human minds, 75; These contacts are more frequent, 35

Spirit of Christ: Ample shield against Satan, 45

Spiritualism: Another name for Witchcraft, 113; Deceives by counterfeiting truth, 114

Star of David. See Witchcraft; Called hexagram or Crest of Solomon, 85

Starhawk, Miriam. See Witchcraft; 63

Stokes, Teri, 89

Subliminal Messages: Found in Beatles and other rock groups, 96

Sun God Ra. See *Witchcraft*
Sutphen, Dick, 98
Sutton, William Josiah, 64, 84, 87, 112, 113, 139, 141, 144, 146

—T—

Table of Contents, 7
Taylor, John, 70, 131
Temple Work: Lucifer discourages, 57
The "One": Claims to be superior to Elohim, 107; Is Lucifer, 107; The Battle of the End, 58
"The Plan": Is coming together, 29; Outline of great Luciferian Conspiracy, 24; Those who resist to be exterminated, 48
Theosophical Society: Created by Helena Petrovna Blavatsky, 23
Timms, Moria, 52
Todd, John, 64, 65, 66, 85, 96, 112, 144, 145; Believed the devil did not exist, 63; Grand Druid on the Council of 13, 63
Transcendental Meditation: To counter spreading demon of Christianity, 74
Trilateral Commission: Co-created by David Rockefeller & Zbigniew Brzezinski, 67; Initiated members of Illuminati, 66; International in membership, 67
Tuella: Channel for the Ashtar Command, 26
Tugwell, Rexford G., 70

—U—

U.S. Supreme Court: Treaty law supersedes domestic law, 72
Uehling, Mark D., 99
Unicorn's Horn: Also known as the Italian Horn, 88; Means you trust the Devil for your finance, 88
United Nations: Will be the new seat of world government, 121

—V—

Valley of Hinnom: Solomon allowed infant sacrifices, 86
Van Orden, Dell, 139
Viereck, John-Alexis, 155
Volker, Paul, 24
Vollenweider, Andreas, 99

—W—

War in Heaven: Raging on earth today, 130; Those with priesthood, valiant, 129; Wrong side meant eternal damnation, 130
Warburg, James, 66
Ward, Rear Admiral Chester, 66
Warner, Christian, 142
Warnke, Mike, 95
Weishaupt, Adam, 65; Created Illuminati May 1, 1776, 65; Outlined "The Plan," 24
White, Charles, 145
Widtsoe, John A., 115, 141
Williams, Hal, 145
Witchcraft: Astrology the cornerstone of, 112; Is a religion, 63; Lucifer, God of witches, 64; Religion of Illuminati, 64; Similar to Eastern beliefs, 63
Witchcraft Bible: Written by Solomon, 85
Wonder Woman: Sign of white magic on forehead, 84
World Court: Genocide Act makes American citizens answerable to the, 72
World Domination: Satan's thirteen-point plan for, 47

—Y—

Yin/Yang: Ancient Chinese symbol for unity, 87
Yogi, Maharishi Mahesh, 75
Young, Brigham, 53, 55, 116, 129, 132

—Z—

Zappa, Frank, 90
Zion: All is well in, 17

DAVID N. BALMFORTH

David N. Balmforth, a native of eastern Idaho, has lived in the Shelley area for much of his life on a small farm overlooking the Snake River. He attended Ricks College for a year and a half before entering the workforce and starting his family.

He married Margaret (Peggy) L. Adams, formerly of Seattle Washington. She is a convert and has served a mission for the Church in Chile. They have seven children.

David has served in many Church positions. In particular he has been active as a Stake Missionary, serving as a Seventy, Ward Mission Leader, Stake Mission Secretary, and as a counselor in the Shelley Idaho, Stake Mission Presidency.

He is an active participant in local and county politics, having served as Precinct Committeeman, County 1st and 2nd vice chairman, and as a delegate to the state convention for his political party.

Brother Balmforth first became aware of the New Age Movement and the dangers it poses by reading *The Hidden Dangers of the Rainbow*, by Christian attorney Constance Cumby. While continuing his investigation and monitoring of this worldwide Satanic organization, he became concerned that there was a large number of Saints who were unaware of the increasing acceptance of many of the occult beliefs embodied in the New Age Movement, and thus the idea for this book was born.